Omoiyari

HarperCollins*Publishers*
1 London Bridge Street
London SE1 9GF
www.harpercollins.co.uk

HarperCollins*Publishers*
Macken House,
39/40 Mayor Street Upper,
Dublin 1, D01 C9W8, Ireland

First published by
HarperCollins*Publishers* 2020

10 9 8 7 6 5 4

A catalogue record of this book is
available from the British Library

ISBN 978-0-00-840762-9

Printed and bound in the UAE

Omoiyari

THE JAPANESE
ART OF COMPASSION

Erin Niimi Longhurst
新美英鈴

Illustrations by Ryo Takemasa 武政諒

 HarperCollins*Publishers*

Contents

Introduction

Introduction

During the 2018 World Cup, after a surprise victory against Colombia, Japanese football fans dominated headlines for reasons other than their country's stellar performance on the pitch: following a historic win (and an excellent excuse to celebrate, if ever there was one), they meticulously cleared up the stadium, collecting litter as a sign of respect for their surroundings as guests.

For those who have been to Japan, stories like this might seem familiar. I've been lucky enough to hear many of them – examples of the spirit of *omoiyari*, the feelings of empathy and compassion that fuel the actions that people take for others. It's demonstrated most clearly in the art of Japanese hospitality, but through various other practices and traditions, too.

Living as we do, in a divisive and rapidly changing world, I felt compelled to write this book, as rather than building walls and becoming too insular, I believe there is something crucial and extremely valuable in sharing perspectives, better understanding others and, in so doing, gaining a deeper understanding of ourselves. This is *omoiyari*.

And what better time to write about the concept of *omoiyari*, and caring for others and the world around us, than at the beginning of a new era? With the abdication of the Emperor Akihito on 30 April 2019, Japan entered a new imperial age, known as *Reiwa* period. *Reiwa* means 'beautiful harmony'. The concept of *wa*, or harmony, is at the very heart of *omoiyari*. So it seems incredibly fitting to be able to explore and better understand these traditions, philosophies and practices during this time.

GOOD DONE TO OTHERS IS GOOD DONE TO ONESELF.

Japanese proverb

What is *Omoiyari?*

It is difficult to define *omoiyari* without first explaining *omoi*, which is a bit of a challenge in itself. There are many homophones in the Japanese language, and the meaning behind words that might sound the same (especially to those who are not native speakers) has to become clear from the context – or, if written, from the *kanji* (the Japanese system of writing that utilises Chinese characters).

A person might be standing in front of you, straining from the weight of a box they have in their arms. They might tell you that the box is *omoi* – and in this context, you'd want to give them a hand with it, as it's a heavy box. But as you might have guessed, this is not a book about heavy Japanese things.

Omoi in the context of this book, reflects the concept of thought. *Omoi* can refer to the way people think, or their feelings, emotions, sentiments or desires. Memories or recollections are *omoide*, which loosely translates to 'thoughts that have come out, or have left'. I have a vivid childhood memory of being caught in the pantry in the middle of the night, jetlagged and elbow-deep in a bag of *kappa ebisen* (shrimp-flavoured crackers) by my grandfather. Rather than giving me the scolding I was bracing myself for, he took the opportunity to eschew a low-sodium diet he was on at the time (imposed by my grandmother and aunts) to join me in the feast. Breaking out the red-bean ice cream, he justified his actions by using the moment to make a good *omoide* with me.

Thoughts, memories and feelings can come and go. Something you have been pondering might suddenly come to you, arriving in your mind like a train pulling into its final destination (*omoitsuku*); and *omoi* can describe not only the thoughts in your mind, but also the way in which you think about things, too.

OMOIYARI
IS A FORM
OF SELFLESS
COMPASSION.

Omoiyari is an extension of this thinking in relation to others – a type of projection. It is the combination of thought and the verb 'to do', but it is more than just thinking about doing something for other people. The simplest way to describe it might be to anticipate the needs of others, but in an altruistic way, imbued with sympathy, empathy – without the expectation of reward or anything in return. Doing something for gain, or with an ulterior motive, is perhaps the complete opposite of *omoiyari* as a concept. *Omoiyari* is a form of selfless compassion: putting yourself in the shoes of others, and from their perspective anticipating their needs – acting in a way that might make them at ease, happy or comfortable. It's about heightening your awareness to the needs of those around you, and acting in a considerate way. In a Japanese restaurant, for example, you'll often find hooks or other ways to stow your bags carefully, so they don't end up scuffed on the floor (or, if you're me, smelling like barbecued meat when you're out having drinks and *yakiniku* skewers with your mates). Not having these things wouldn't necessarily detract from your dining experience. However, being taken care of, and having someone anticipate the fact that you might not want that handbag you saved up for dragged along the floor gives you a nice feeling.

Why is this important though? Why must we anticipate the needs of others? If someone wants something, why don't they simply ask for it? Why can't we just communicate? These are all completely valid questions. Open communication is extremely important, as is asking for help when you need it.

But I think *omoiyari* is important because, on a larger scale, we need to try to understand perspectives and worldviews that might be outside of or in contrast to our own. Even if we disagree with them, there is always value in expanding our minds and trying to make sense of it all. There is a Japanese proverb that is particularly fitting

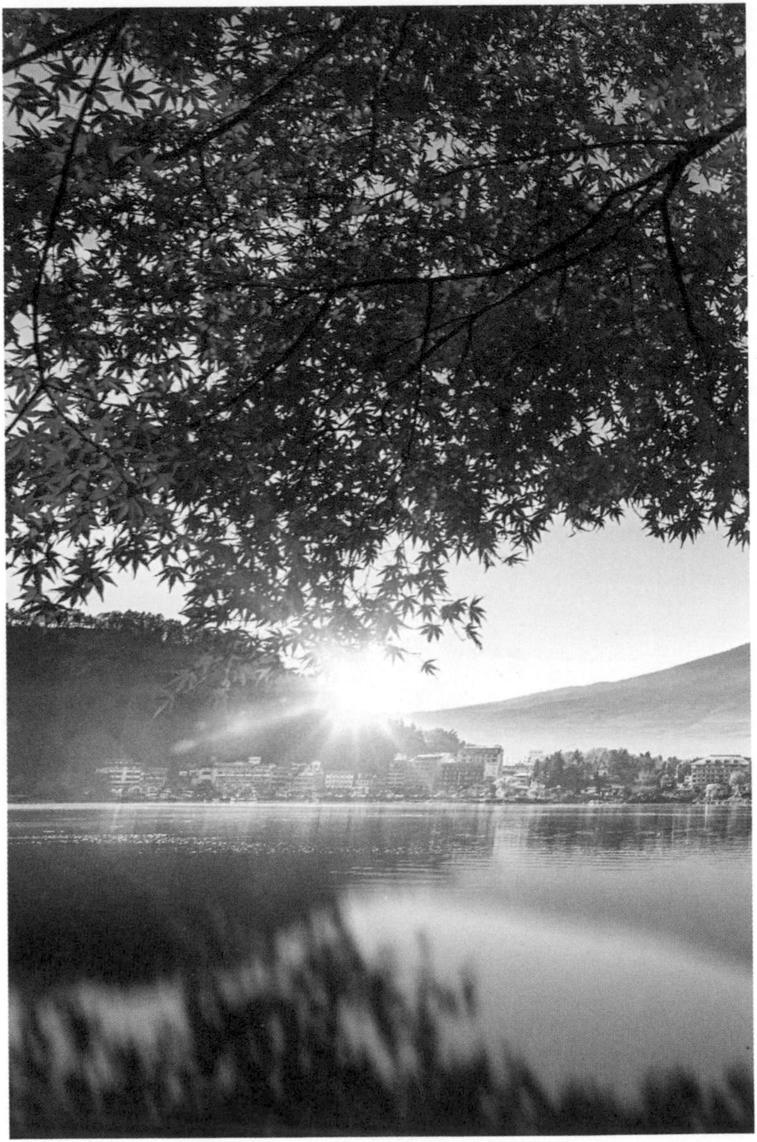

here: 'A frog in a well cannot conceive of the ocean'. I've always hated frogs, and it's only just occurred to me that this proverb might be the reason why – I wouldn't want to assume my perspective is the only one, or the correct one. *Omoiyari* might help you to keep an open mind, but with the added benefit of being kinder and more considerate to others in an attempt to make your environment a better place.

What can *omoiyari* provide?

The cynic in me might argue that a culture of *omoiyari* came out of necessity in Japan – vital in keeping the peace for an island nation that, for 220 years, was isolated from the rest of the world. But I'm not a cynical person. My favourite part of Christmas Day is never the opening of presents (the performance element scares me. What if I hate it, and my face gives it away? It's all the reasons why I've never liked improv), but about choosing and wrapping a thoughtful gift for someone that I think they might like, find useful or enjoy. Doing something that might make someone else's day a little bit better, make them happier, even if it's just making them more comfortable, is really such a joy. I don't know if anything is more life-affirming than that.

What does *omoiyari* look like?

In order to care for others, you must first care for yourself. In order to anticipate the needs of others – to empathise – you must learn to recognise feelings within yourself, and understand what makes you tick. That's why I've called the first part of this book '*Omoi*', with a focus on how various philosophies, traditions and practices can help you to be mindful, respectful to your surroundings and to express yourself. Part One is about getting to know yourself better, whether that's by being less wasteful, finding a system of organisation or even appreciating the beauty in the most mundane objects.

My first book, *Japonisme,* was all about finding contentment through different Japanese philosophies and practices – things like *ikigai, wabi-sabi, shinrin-yoku* (forest bathing) and calligraphy. With *Omoiyari,* I want to think more about the art of compassion – how we can bring joy into our own lives by bringing about happiness in the lives of others.

I want to encourage you all to be kind to yourselves. This might involve taking the time to perfect a craft, or pursue a passion that is wholly your own, or for your own enjoyment or benefit. The joy that comes from mastering a craft is something I learned from my *Jiji,* my Japanese grandfather. A shrewd businessman, and also a temple elder, he devoted a lot of his time to painting, cooking and other hobbies and mindful practices, despite a hectic work schedule, the demands of running a large business, as well as an active family life. They helped him to clear his mind and be creative in his thinking in other areas of his life. My aunt Taeko took up tea ceremony (*chado*) as a way to carve out time to pursue something that was outside the constraints of her job or family life – something that allowed her to connect with nature and her environment, and to appreciate specific moments of the year and the changing of the seasons. Growing up with these examples of ways in which to connect with ourselves has been invaluable to me. I find it particularly through cooking mindfully – nothing gives me greater clarity, comfort or joy than putting together all the parts of a meal. It's my way of showing affection to myself.

My focus for Part Two, *Omoiyari,* is about how you bring this to others – through harmonious living, selflessness, paying respect where it's due and showing appreciation. This might be done through gift-giving, cooking a meal for a loved one, celebrating key

moments and even things like *origami*. *Omoiyari* is about extending your thoughts to others, not through words, but through action, and putting them into practice.

Striving to be more sympathetic, empathetic and considerate requires a degree of faith, and a healthy serving of trust in others. For some, this might mean letting their guard down and being vulnerable. This can yield some incredible results – like ordering *omakase* style (literally 'I'll leave it up to you') at a restaurant. By putting the selection of dishes and ingredients completely in the hands of a chef – a virtual stranger – you do run the risk of getting a few dishes that might not be quite to your taste. However, it can also open your eyes to something completely new – unknown flavours and textures that can transform the way you think about food altogether. When you place your trust and faith in them, they can take you on a journey; you gain insight into their history, their likes and dislikes, their world and their vision. Then, having broadened your frame of reference, you can cast your net wider in the future. It's often an incredibly intimate experience, but the spirit of *omoiyari*, which is an integral part of an *omakase*-style meal, results in a deep connection – one that is based on mutual respect.

Omoiyari is not about ulterior motives, furthering a business prospect or taking a romantic relationship to another level. It's bigger than that – perhaps karmic – but I like to think it's about leaving a place you've been in either the same way or better than you found it. It's about respect – for yourself, for the ones around you and for the environment, too. And through this little book, I hope to help you achieve this – because even the smallest of considerate actions can make a world of difference.

Part 1:

Omoi
思い

If you look in a dictionary to find a direct translation of the word '*omoi*', you'll find 'thought', 'feeling', 'emotion' and 'sentiment'. But it's knowing and understanding these within ourselves which allows us to be empathetic, bestowing kind actions and thoughts onto others – compassion through the art of *omoiyari*.

I felt it important to highlight the role that our own thoughts, desires and passions play in this process. It's not possible to be self*less* without understanding the self; it's impossible to be kind to others if we haven't had the experience of being kind to ourselves.

In many respects, Japanese culture is hierarchical. This becomes especially apparent in a business context, or in any situation where *keigo*, or honorific speech, is used. Having said that, it also places significant importance on mutual respect, particularly inter-generationally. Celebration of Respect for the Aged Day, for example, is emblematic of the loyalty and appreciation shown to the elderly, and what can be learned from them, in terms of the experience and wisdom they have gained through the passage of time.

The importance of mutual respect, and conveying it, is not stated explicitly in Japanese culture, but performed through actions. The strict etiquette and cultural customs around body language, greetings, even things as seemingly unimportant as bathing, business cards and writing letters, can reveal so much about the way people interact, and give insight into a larger worldview.

This part of the book, *'Omoi'*, focuses very much on the self – activities and practices to encourage you to see things differently, set new habits and get in touch with your creative side. The aim is to help you find joy, satisfaction and appreciation in your life, whether through changing your mindset about what you use or consume, making your surroundings beautiful or taking a greater level of care in what you do.

The first chapter, *'Mottainai'* (a sense of regret over waste, or for things not meeting their full potential), focuses on how we can make what we have go further. I have a British father and a Japanese mother and was lucky enough to get to know and be very close to both sets of grandparents. All four grew up during the Second World War, and although on opposing sides, a culture of conservation was something they all had in common. It's becoming more apparent now that these values are still significant, especially as sustainability is more important than ever. Respecting what we have, and ensuring that we don't take it for granted, is at the heart of the *mottainai* philosophy.

My *Jiji* (Japanese for grandfather) was a huge influence in my life. He was the man responsible for shaping my understanding of the world. As chairman and CEO of a huge global corporation, he was a formidable and impressive man. I got to see and be inspired by his sharp mind, his business acumen, strong leadership skills and decision making. But I was truly blessed because I was also able to see the side of him that made this possible – a softer side, and one that was very spiritual. Observing him in his natural habitat on the weekends, as a temple elder and outside the hustle and bustle of Tokyo, I came to understand the practices and traditions he valued so highly. As an adult, I find myself employing some of those same techniques and practices in order to find stillness and a sense of calm, even at times when it can be a challenge.

During the weekend, he would go to our family home in Kamakura, a small coastal city just over an hour away from Tokyo. Kamakura is the former de facto capital of Japan and is steeped in history. Most notably, it is the home of the Tsurugaoka Hachimangū temple, where he spent a lot of his time.

In addition to painting and gardening, one of my clearest memories of him as I was growing up was how he spent his weekends cleaning the house. I distinctly remember rolling around the house during my school holidays, weakened by the oppressive Japanese summer heat, wondering whether or not I should offer help to *Jiji* as he carefully and tenderly took a straw broom across the *engawa* (a veranda next to the *tatami*-matted room). I'd often end up playing with my cousins or picking fights with my little sister, rather than offering assistance. It didn't make sense to me at the time – a cleaner came to the house fairly frequently, we weren't allowed shoes indoors and it never seemed *that* dirty.

What I've come to understand since is that making his home *kirei*, or clean and beautiful, was less about physically sweeping the dust away, but more about a performative ritual. The importance of the act came from the power it had to clear his mind, show respect and gratitude for the home he had worked so hard for and appreciation for my grandmother (who I call *Baba*), who helped him to raise their three children, and who was his main collaborator in the life that they built together. It is this mindset and approach that I will describe in greater detail in the chapter about cleanliness and organisation, or *kirei*.

Jiji practised mindfulness through his cleaning ritual. Not unlike the way in which some Japanese army generals practise *ikebana*, or the art of flower arranging, to clear their minds as they strategise, *Jiji* cleared his mind and thought about his next move as he swept.

He was also diligent, and *teinei* (precise, measured and thoughtful*)* in his approach – he brought the same tenacity and energy that made him so successful in the business world to the pursuit of his hobbies, too, whether painting, composing *haiku* or preparing your favourite meal if he knew you were visiting. He had a way of making you feel incredibly special; but the real skill lay in

making so many people feel that way. There were over 2,000 people at his funeral, and each of them had a story about him to share with my family. While he was a naturally charismatic person, a lot of this was learned – he was able to influence and build relationships through listening and by paying attention to the details. In the chapter about being *teinei*, I expand upon this further. In the final chapter of *'Omoi'*, I explore the style and design phenomenon of *zakka* – finding the extraordinary in the mundane and ordinary. *Zakka* is about being an active curator in your home and, by extension, in your life. For my appreciation of this, I have to thank the women in my life – my mother, grandmother and aunts. Whether through calligraphy, *ikebana*, tea ceremony or cooking, their influence gave me an awareness of the possibilities that humble, everyday objects and activities can bring.

In calligraphy, a simple brush and ink, once on canvas, can reveal hesitations, uncertainties and even the state of mind of the artist at a given moment to an expert eye. An arrangement of flowers can reveal so much about the changing of the seasons. And the acts of chopping, slicing, heating and whisking can transform even the most modest of ingredients into a meal that has its own narrative, creating a powerful story.

Many of the philosophies, practices, tips and traditions I share in *Omoi* are about more than the sum of their parts. One of my favourite Japanese proverbs and sayings is *kachou fuugetsu*. The *kanji* characters for this saying are those for flower, bird, wind and moon – 花鳥風月 – but the meaning behind this sentiment is about experiencing the beauties of nature and, in the process of doing so, learning about yourself. Practising *shinrin-yoku* (forest bathing) might not be so accessible on a day-to-day basis for many of us. But my ambition with *omoi* is to encourage this feeling of learning and connecting with yourself, through adapting your mindset and how you interact with your space, as well as how you approach tasks. It's about experiencing the beauty of the natural world, but also the world we make for ourselves, enabling us to make that connection with ourselves on a deeper level. Through this, we are able to build strength and be the version of us that we'd like to be – becoming better equipped and able to share this feeling and goodwill with others.

If *Omoiyari* as a concept is about empathy and the art of compassion, then *omoi* is about getting in touch with our thought processes and passions. It's crucial to be able to know ourselves, before we share, dedicate and devote time to helping others. It's about understanding our thoughts, feelings and emotions, as well as harnessing, exploring and unlocking the potential of our sentimental side.

MOTTAINAI

勿体無い

Avoiding Waste

GOOD FORTUNE CAN EXIST IN WHAT GETS LEFT BEHIND.

Japanese proverb

I wish there was a Japanese word to describe the lies that parents tell their children to cajole them into doing things, because it's a truly universal phenomenon – a global conspiracy, where even the most unimaginative of grown-ups are transformed into skilful storytellers in an attempt to get their offspring to toe the line.

As a child, I was told a story about a rice farmer. The industrious rice farmer in question would wake up early to work in the fields, day after day, just so Erin would be able to enjoy a delicious bowl of white, fluffy rice at dinner. But, for every single grain of rice that Erin *didn't* scrape from the side of her bowl and eat, this tireless (and extremely emotionally fragile) farmer would shed a tear. To this day, I can't bear to leave any food, and so my family's attempts to instil a fear of waste – or the feeling of '*mottainai*' – in me was a great success.

'*Mottainai!*' is a phrase you might commonly hear if you've left food on your plate (and heartlessly made a farmer cry). However, it's not just limited to the dinner table. You might also hear it if you're not able to get anyone else to take your seats for a show you were meant to be going to, or when you have to get rid of a dress you bought but never wore (which serves you right for getting overexcited in the sales).

The concept of *mottainai* has roots in Shinto animism – the belief that *kami* (spirits) inhabit all things. In order to honour these spirits, you take care of objects, respect them and aim to preserve their dignity where possible. *Mottainai* is about continuing to hope – rather than discarding unnecessarily, or giving up on something, it's about coming up with solutions and ways of making things last.

Reduce, reuse, repair and recycle

The Japanese aversion to being wasteful means that many cultural practices and traditions have developed as a result. In order to make sure that objects meet their full potential and remain useful, there is an emphasis on reusing, repairing and recycling, so reducing the number of things that are discarded.

As a phrase, *mottainai* has been appropriated globally, mostly by environmentalists. Nobel Prize-winning social and environmental activist Wangari Maathai used the word during a United Nations summit on climate change: 'Even at personal level, we can all reduce, reuse and recycle – what is embraced as *mottainai* in Japan, a concept that also calls us to express gratitude, to respect and to avoid wastage.'[1]

Gratitude and respect towards objects are implied when something is *mottainai* – it is often a type of apology, an expression of regret and an acknowledgment that an opportunity was lost in some way. Once something is *mottainai*, it might be too late – so one might take pains to ensure that things *do* meet their full potential, for as long as possible. Things might be repaired, preserved, given another chance or a new lease of life, to further their usefulness rather than being needlessly discarded.

The concept of *mottainai* is closely linked to that of *wabi-sabi* – a Japanese aesthetic and worldview that promotes the acceptance of transience, impermanence and imperfection, and the beauty of the journey and passage of time.

Kintsugi 金継ぎ

Perhaps one of the most visually stunning ways in which objects are repaired and cared for is through the art of *kintsugi*, where broken ceramics are repaired using gold- or silver-coloured lacquer. Not only does it increase longevity for the particular object in question, but in *chado* (Japanese tea ceremony) it makes that object more desirable or interesting as a result of its perceived flaws.

The cracks are highlighted by the lacquer, which becomes a key feature – a memorable event or obstacle in the life cycle of the item. The gilded cracks are illuminated, but with dignity and honour, and the beauty is that the object still retains its usefulness and serves its purpose.

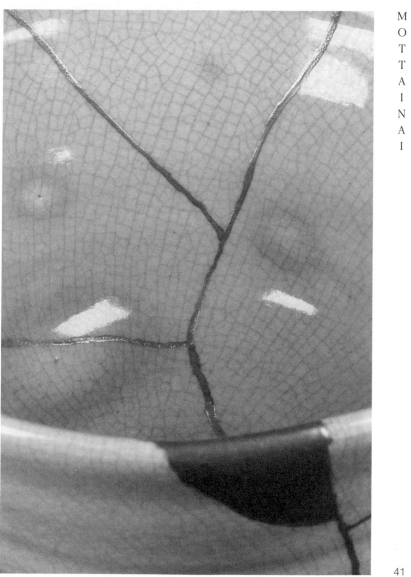

The Hospital for Stuffed Toys

In Osaka, there is a hospital for toys. The *nuigurumi byouin* (stuffed-toy hospital) offers a sanctuary – a place where plush playthings can be cared for, restuffed and repaired, their owners safe in the knowledge that their most prized possessions will get the tender care that they need and be treated with respect and affection.

Clothing and textiles

There are some artisanal techniques surrounding the maintenance of clothing, whether preserving and extending the life of fabric or repairing garments in an aesthetically pleasing way.

Boro ぼろ

Boro is a type of clothing made through patchwork – deriving from the word '*boro-boro*', which refers to something that is tattered, or in need of repair. *Boro* clothing was worn mostly by peasants in the nineteenth century, with items of clothing that had been worn and repaired being passed down through generations. *Boro* clothing was usually dyed in an indigo hue. In a modern, post-Second World War era, it was seen to be symbolic of Japan's impoverished past, but there has recently been a revival of items in this style. *Boro* clothing was born from necessity – fabrics like cotton or silk were not readily available to those who were not in the upper classes – and its humble origins truly capture the spirit of *mottainai*, where things are preserved and passed on to others and nothing is wasted.

43

Sakiori 裂織

Sakiori is a type of woven fabric, made from scraps or residual materials and held together using yarn. The word is a combination of the term '*saki*', to tear, and '*ori*', to weave together. Objects made using this woven fabric include rugs, *kotatsu* (a type of low table covered with a *futon*) covers or informal *kimono obis* (belts).

Sashiko 刺し子

Sashiko is a type of decorative stitching, used to reinforce materials that have been impacted by wear and tear. *Sashiko* sewing techniques are often geometric in style, making the repairs look aesthetically pleasing through the use of 'little stitches' (the literal translation of the term). In a spirit similar to *kintsugi*, in addition to mending any damage, *sashiko* stitching adds an element of embellishment, highlighting any repairs made using a white or red thread.

The different stitch styles are often inspired by nature – design elements like *tate-waku* (rising steam), *amime* (fishing nets), *yarai* (bamboo fence), as well as employing geometric shapes like checks, diamonds and striped patterns.

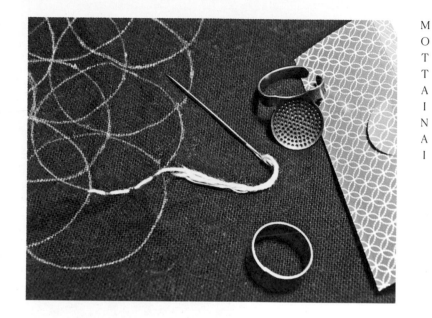

Ingredients and food

The essence of *mottainai* impacts the Japanese attitude to food preparation, ingredients and meals. Examples include using *okara*, the soybean by-product of tofu or soy milk production or *sake kasu* (by-product of *sake*) to season and marinate fish or pickle vegetables.

In order to avoid food wastage or being *mottainai* with your food, one approach is to only eat until you are 80 per cent full (*hara hachi bu*). Other ways to prolong or reuse ingredients might be to transform them, as, for example, when making your own *furikake* – a Japanese seasoning that you might have with rice, vegetables or fish. It's also a fun way to flavour popcorn.

Homemade *furikake* is extremely easy to prepare and is often made after people have used *katsuobushi* (also known as *bonito* flakes, which are dried, fermented and smoked tuna flakes) to make *dashi* stock. It's incredibly easy to use, too; *furikake* means to 'sprinkle on top', and that's exactly what you do with this seasoning, to add a little bit of depth and umami flavour to a dish.

Furikake

30g *katsuobushi* (*bonito* flakes)
2 tablespoons black sesame seeds
2 tablespoons white sesame seeds
1 teaspoon salt
½ teaspoon sugar
2 sheets *nori* (seaweed)

1. If you have used the *katsuobushi* flakes to make stock, make sure these are properly strained. *Katsuobushi* is often sold in the form of flakes, thin shavings – once used in stock, the flakes tend to clump together. In a frying pan, cook the strained *katsuobushi* (*bonito* flakes) until the liquid has evaporated, and the *katsuobushi* has started to become dry and begun to flake again. Place this on a tray.

2. In the same dry pan, lightly toast the sesame seeds over a low heat. Remove and place in a bowl to cool.

3. Once the sesame seeds have cooled, add them, along with the salt, sugar and nori, to the tray with the *katsuobushi*. Once everything has cooled, you can store this mixture in a jar. Sprinkle over rice, fish, popcorn – whatever takes your fancy.

Applying *mottainai* in everyday life

— Clothes swap

I'm lucky enough to have made friends who are roughly the same size as me, so if one of us is going to a big event, rather than buying a new dress (which may never be worn again), we've come up with a clothes-swap system. It reduces the amount of space taken up in our wardrobes, as well as the hit on our wallets – it's a win–win!

— Compost

My English grandparents are keen gardeners, so I learned from them to compost food waste wherever possible. There is so much goodness that can be returned to the ground from your kitchen food waste. If this is an option available to you where you live, take advantage of it.

— Meal planning

One of the easiest ways to stick to a balanced diet, reduce food waste and save money is through meal planning. This doesn't have to be boring or uninspiring; in fact, it can be an absolute pleasure – you just have to be realistic: are you really going to want a fruit cup and a light salad for lunch on a Friday afternoon or might you want something that feels like a treat? If you're going to end up wasting your packed lunch and heading to the pub with your colleagues, then be honest with yourself – and reduce waste in the process.

What can we learn from *mottainai?*

The Japanese *mottainai* philosophy encourages us to see the potential in things, to find appreciation in and respect them. It also inspires us to cherish the things we have, to take care of them, and cultivate them if necessary. It's not a negative emotion, but one that is thought-provoking and even awe-inspiring. In a world where we are rapidly running out of resources and urgently need to change our habits to preserve and protect our environment, *mottainai* can encourage us to be more sustainable. Respecting our belongings, extending the life of things and reducing our waste can not only benefit our planet, but provide us with a sense of respect and gratitude, too.

02

KIREI

綺麗

Cleanliness and Organisation

HOW MUCH DOES HE LACK HIMSELF WHO MUST HAVE MANY THINGS?

Sen no Rikyu

In Japan, you can use the same word – *kirei* – to mean 'clean' as well as 'beautiful'. Cleanliness and organisation are highly significant in Japanese culture, not only for yourself and your home, but in public spaces, too. Visitors to Japan might notice that communal spaces, like streets, parks and train stations, are kept clean, despite the fact that there are fewer public rubbish bins. There is a cultural aversion to littering and mess – largely linked to ideas around purity.

The concept of purity is central to the Shinto tradition and belief system, and purification rituals play a key role in this. When I lived in Tokyo as a child, I went to a local *hoikuen*, or nursery school. In addition to the usual nursery-school activities you might encounter elsewhere, we also had a set time for cleaning up after ourselves. While this isn't uncommon elsewhere, in Japan it is taken a little further with the use of brooms, vacuum cleaners and so on. Pupils, rather than hired cleaning staff, are required to take responsibility for the maintenance and upkeep of their classrooms in a way that goes beyond the superficial. This is not only a sign of respect for their surroundings, but also instils a sense of shared accountability and care for communal spaces.

In addition to the cultural and religious angles, however, there is also a purely practical explanation. As a small island, and particularly in densely populated cities like Tokyo, the clever use of space is crucial. A clean and organised space not only helps you make your square footage go further, but as can be learned from Shinto traditions and practices, has the added benefit of helping to clear your mind too.

At Home

A clean home – one in which you are aware and conscious of your things, and able to keep track of them effectively – is one of the simplest ways to avoid that feeling of *mottainai*. I find that having a clean and well-organised home, free from clutter, can also help with concentration – which is becoming even more important as remote working has become the norm for many people.

The simplest way to ensure you have a clean home is not to put things off or assume that you will get to something later. If you've used a plate, wash it right away – be diligent, rather than just popping it into the sink. The presence of a single plate in the sink has a kind of magnetic power – and soon enough you'll notice used bowls, spoons and chopsticks adding to the pile and creating clutter. Think about it as taking responsibility for your actions – leaving something behind, even something as small as one plate, puts the burden on someone else. It might be a friend, a family member, a housemate, even your future self. By conscientiously picking up after yourself, you're showing a sign of respect, not only to the object, but also to the people who share your environment.

Change never happens overnight, so it's not about punishing yourself if you don't become a clean freak after reading this chapter. Think about the concept of *kaizen* – very small improvements made over a long period of time to bring about efficiency and change. You don't have to alphabetise your spice rack just yet, but if you make a commitment to ensuring that you always keep the sink clean, you'll start noticing and wanting to respect other elements of your space, too.

Osouji 大掃除

One way to ensure your home is *kirei* is to take part in *osouji* at least once a year. *Osouji* is an annual ritual in which people will do a big deep-clean of their home, in preparation for the year ahead. *Osouji* rituals were believed to have originated from the tradition of *susu-harai,* dusting the soot away in the temples. According to tradition, a ritual deep-clean to purify the home created a welcoming environment for *Toshigami* (deities) in the New Year.

But *osouji* is not just about giving all your surfaces a good wipe. It's the time of year when you attend to all the neglected areas of your home. You might pay extra attention to your windowsills, for example, dust off your ceiling fans, vents and grates – traditionally, it's when you cleaned out your hearth, for example. *Osouji* also allows you to reflect on your past year in a mindful way, putting things behind you (if necessary) and preparing for a fresh start. Even if you are lucky enough to employ a cleaner, I think *osouji* should be undertaken at least once a year by you and the people who actually live in a given environment – not only so you will appreciate your space and the objects that fill it, but also because de-cluttering is very personal and only you can decide what needs to stay and what needs to go.

The reason why *osouji* is so effective is that it requires you, to a point, to dismantle everything. Over the course of the year, you can take a piecemeal approach to cleaning, by focusing on specific rooms. With *osouji*, it's better to tear it all down – empty all your cupboards into the middle of the living room, take everything out of those boxes and embrace the temporary chaos. Once the job is done, you will feel like a phoenix rising from the ashes. During *osouji*, it's important to throw yourself into the process entirely. There is a Japanese proverb that goes: 'The hunter who chases two hares catches neither' – *this* is the bunny you need to be focusing on.

Osouji: My Top Five Tips

1. Put it in the calendar.

The *osouji* ritual at the end of the year is effective because you've carved out time to make it a priority. Traditionally, it took place around 13 December, but these days, it's commonly done around the 29 or 30 December, in preparation for New Year's Eve.

2. Stop holding on to things.

We've all been guilty of it: holding on to things – waiting for the right occasion to wear something or not liking a specific gift, but keeping it because we don't want to offend the person who gave it to us. Give yourself a time limit or a deadline with those items and remember to appreciate the thought behind the gift, but don't feel bad. The same goes for clothing. It's time to make space.

3. It's a team effort.

Many hands make light work, and it's important for everyone who lives in the space to contribute to its maintenance and upkeep. As a child, I'd been putting off cleaning a wardrobe of mine for a long time, despite constant reminders from my mother to do so. Eventually, she took things into her own hands and got rid of its entire contents to make room for some winter coats. At the time, I was traumatised, but it taught me a valuable lesson. I wasn't respecting my space, nor was I demonstrating care and respect for the objects inside it. Understandably, my mother took that as a sign of my indifference. It's important to take stock of your possessions, but also show your respect to the people you live with. Take responsibility for your possessions and the space that you share with the people you care about.

4. Timing is everything.

Make sure you allocate enough time for the annual *osouji* ritual, but also for cleaning your space on a weekly basis. As a rule of thumb for a standard clean, allocate one hour per room per person who lives there. For example, I live alone in a studio apartment, so I spend an hour cleaning the bathroom, an hour on my bedroom alcove and an hour on my living room/kitchen area every couple of weeks (cleaning up after myself every day in the meantime).

5. Treat yourself.

For the annual *osouji*, the big treat at the end will be all the New Year celebrations, but if you do a clean of any kind, allocate yourself some sort of treat that you don't allow yourself usually. I don't have a TV, and am more of a reader, but when I'm cleaning, I usually have a guilty-pleasure reality TV show on in the background. Rewarding yourself with something you don't usually do makes the occasion a bit more exciting and special.

De-cluttering: what to get rid of

When it comes to organising your space, it's important to think about the things you are holding on to, which are contributing to clutter. I tend to do quarterly de-clutterings of my wardrobe and cupboards. These are the easiest things I've found to streamline:

— Clothes

If it doesn't fit, and hasn't done for a while, it goes. I also like to do the coat-hanger trick: after a big *osouji*, I'll hang everything up so that the sharp end of the coat hanger faces me as I look at the rail. Whenever I wear something, I'll hang it back up, with the sharp end facing away from me, towards the back of the wardrobe. Then, every few months, I'll take a look, and if I haven't worn something for a while, I'll reconsider whether or not I keep it.

— Cosmetics

Make-up and cosmetics have an expiry date, so don't hold on to them for too long. I'm very guilty of this, especially if I've bought a specific eyeshadow for a special occasion (like festivals, or fancy dress). Steer clear of those hotel miniatures, too – they always end up at the back of the drawer. Find another use for them, like potentially donating unused ones.

— Books

There is a word, *tsundoku*, which refers to books you've purchased and don't end up reading. As someone who just spent a small fortune shipping her books over, I can appreciate this – but I also think books are things that should be shared. If you read something, and think it would be enjoyed by someone else, share it with them. I like to include a note with mine, mentioning my favourite things about the book, and why I think they might enjoy it.

— Kitchen equipment

I have a few appliances in the kitchen I'd be hard pressed to cook without, and it's taken me a couple of years to whittle down and streamline this list. Same thing with cutlery – wooden spoons are a key culprit when it comes to kitchen clutter. A useful way of getting around this is by visualising the most complicated meal you might make on a semi-regular basis, and what equipment and cutlery you would need to prepare it. For anything else, you can beg, borrow or steal at a later date – you don't need to own it or have it taking up space unnecessarily.

— Furniture

Because I've always lived in cities where space is at a premium, I've learned not to be overly sentimental about furniture. Inherited pieces, whether from the family or in rented/shared accommodation, can often lead to clutter. Donating might be an option, as might upcycling; I once made a stool out of an old washing machine drum, giving it a new lease of life.

5S Methodology

The 5S methodology was developed in Japan as a way to help people organise their workspaces, but I find it has very practical applications for the home as well. It's based on optimising manufacturing processes, and the five Ss of the title refer to five words that outline a process for efficiency:

1. *Seiri* – sorting

I have friends and family members who are sticklers for hygiene, but their houses aren't 'clean' because there is a lot of mess. *Seiri* is about sorting, organising and discarding. From a practical perspective, it's about eliminating obstacles, reducing distraction and knowing where things are.

2. *Seiton* – sequence

Now you've got rid of excess, you need to find and apply a way of organising what's left. It might be as simple as putting the plates and pans that you use most frequently at the front of the cupboards or organising your wardrobe based on occasion, rather than item, but it involves imposing an order or a plan to make things as efficient and practical for the *real* you, rather than an imagined version of yourself. For example, while I would like to be the person who wears sequinned dresses and stilettos more frequently, I've organised my drawers so that my leggings and trainers are the most easily accessible things.

3. *Seiso* – shine

This refers to the cleaning, inspecting and polishing of your items. It might be repairing any chipped bowls with *kintsugi* or taking your winter coats to the dry cleaners.

4. *Seikestu* – structure

Once you've developed a system of ordering, you need to set a structure to support it. This is all about scheduling and maintenance. So you've organised your wardrobe based on season, but how often do you revisit this? Monthly? Quarterly? Weekly? Put a structure in place, ideally one that others with whom you share your space can understand.

5. *Shitsuke* – self-discipline

This is about making the habit stick, and ensuring that you follow through. The system you develop might require a little tweaking, so if you aren't able to stick to it, do some digging to establish why that is and how you can make it simpler to do so.

At the Temple

Harae is the term for ritual purification in Shinto. Visiting a shrine, particularly at New Year, was a big part of my childhood, and something I still do every time I go to Japan.

On approaching a shrine, you bow your head as you enter or go under the *torii* (gate). Before coming face to face with the deity (within the shrine) you go to the *temizuya* – a water pavilion. You then pick up one of the ladles, filling it with water using your right hand. You empty the ladle over your left hand, then repeat the process with the opposite hand, too, both to clean it and symbolically purify your body and mind with the *temizu* ceremony.

At Work

The concept of *kirei* is also pertinent where it relates to your office or workspace. Being mindful not only about your own space, but shared workspaces, is important. It symbolises the respect you have for the work you do as well as the respect you have for those with whom you share your space – your colleagues and those working around you.

For many of us, these lines can get blurred as increasingly more of us work from home. For me, the division between work and home is crucial. As someone who has spent a long time working from home for much of my career, I know that you can't be productive without carving out this space. If you can, try to reserve a designated space for work. And try not to work from bed.

In many Japanese companies, employees will participate in the year-end *osouji* cleaning ritual, to prepare for the year ahead (and finally clear out that tray of receipts that we all occasionally battle with).

In the Wider World

Keeping things *kirei* doesn't only apply to the spaces you call your own; it's about all the spaces you encounter and includes the wider world too. We can all do our bit in taking responsibility, whether by picking up after ourselves, organising a neighbourhood clean-up or teaching others better habits. In 2016, in a bid to bring more tourists to the French capital, Japanese tour guides in Paris began cleaning up the streets. Eventually, the Paris tourism association funded the initiative in part.[2]

Respect for shared and communal spaces is about gratitude. In terms of what can be learned about keeping your surroundings *kirei*, it is about being accountable and taking ownership, and leaving a space better than how you found it. We can all do our part to help.

03

TEINEI

丁寧

Polite Conscientiousness

ONE WHO SMILES RATHER THAN RAGES IS THE STRONGER.

Japanese proverb

Any time I receive anything from my Aunt Taeko – whether it's a letter, a gift or even something that she's borrowed – it's invariably a thing of beauty. She has excellent penmanship, always uses exquisite stationery, folds things with care and is a dab hand at wrapping. To me, she is the embodiment of doing things *teinei* – with grace and attention to detail. And while over twenty years of being a practitioner of Japanese tea ceremony is definitely a contributing factor, being *teinei* is also a cultural trait.

Teinei is about politeness and respect – doing things with patience, grace and care. It can refer to the method or attitude with which things are done, but it also extends to etiquette – paying attention to the little details. It's about doing things for others with precision and consideration, meticulously. Say you are writing some thank-you cards, for instance: sure, you can write a similar message in each one, then send them off, and you get the message across; however, if you did it *teinei,* you'd think about the pen you'd like to use, and how to personalise your message for each recipient, so that they get a sense of how grateful you are, and how they made you feel. It's about forethought and going the extra mile, not rushing through things.

Teinei can involve getting in touch with your creative side – but it is aspirational, too. Not all of us are talented artists, or natural creators, but being *teinei* encourages you to make space for that side of yourself as well. When we are children, we are encouraged to make art, and explore that side of ourselves, but in adulthood there aren't that many spaces to be creative unless it's how you earn your living.

It's an ever-evolving process, and it won't always be a success. But anyone who has ever been on the receiving end of a hand-knitted scarf, a song, or baked goods will know how wonderful it feels to have someone create and put their energy into something for you – even if it isn't quite to your taste (and is *arigata-meiwaku** to receive!).

Teinei in *Chado* – Japanese Tea Ceremony

The art of *chado* lies in a series of prescribed movements, a demonstration of care and hospitality based on purity, tranquillity, harmony and respect (see p.122 for more on this ritual). Taeko decided to pursue *chado* in her free time as a way to connect with herself, as well as take stock of the changing seasons around her. Being devoted to her hobby and craft, these values also impact her day-to-day life, and she sets an example to me that I very much aspire to.

One story that is often told at family get-togethers is about an occasion when Taeko and my uncle were babysitting me when I was around three years old. They decided to visit some friends, with me in tow, and were amused to find that, on arrival, I greeted them formally (sitting *seiza*-style, on the ground). As a sign of respect, I bowed deeply to them, and precociously took it upon myself to thank them for their hospitality by bestowing on them a gift – a packet of opened and half-used curry powder (my favourite food).

While not executed perfectly (a case of *arigata-meiwaku** for my aunt and uncle), it was a toddler's attempt at being a polite, thoughtful guest – of being *teinei*.

Arigata-meiwaku

A Japanese portmanteau to describe an act that someone does for you which, while rooted in good intentions, potentially overcomplicates things. It is a sort of misplaced kindness, but due to social convention, you are obliged to thank them for it, even though it might have caused you additional hassle. Perhaps you're not a fan of a particular brand of tea, for example, but you don't want to be wasteful, so you keep using it. Just when you are about to finish it, however, a well-intentioned person notices that you're running out, and buys you a fresh box of the same tea, continuing the cycle of mediocre tea drinking. You're grateful for the thought, but it's also mildly irritating.

In tea ceremony, every action is done with deliberation and precision. The difficulty is in making it look easy. Guests are given the most advantageous seat (next to the *tokonoma* – alcove – where art and *ikebana* flower arrangements are displayed). Being *teinei* involves setting high standards and adhering to them. What we can learn from tea ceremony is thinking about the small details. Next time you host an event, think beyond the food and what time people will arrive and be served. What about the atmosphere and experience? How can you make the place settings beautiful? What do guests have in common, and how might you seat them based on interest?

Being *Teinei* in Conversation

Politeness in Japan extends beyond action, and into words, too. As a sign of respect, people speak differently in a customer-service or business setting, using *keigo*, in which language takes on a respectful quality and honorifics. You'd use *keigo* when you are speaking to older people or a distinguished person, and in the workplace.

My key takeaway here is to approach every conversation or interaction respectfully, no matter who you are speaking to. Even when you are dealing with a frustrating situation, it's far more effective to appeal with kindness, rather than anger. Being respectful in content and tone and speaking with precision is almost always the best way to approach things.

Sumimasen – the Most Useful Word in the Japanese Language

If you only remember one word when travelling to Japan, then I would highly recommend that it's '*sumimasen*', which encompasses several things. *Sumimasen* can be used to get someone's attention, particularly if you are disturbing/distracting them in some way (similar to 'excuse me'). It can also be used to say 'I'm sorry', but also to acknowledge the trouble or care that someone has made on your behalf, like in the situation below:

Picture the scene: in a café, Erin orders a cappuccino. Shortly after, a drink is placed in front of her, but it is tea, rather than coffee.

Erin: [to the waiter] **Sumimasen!** *I think there has been a mistake, I ordered a coffee.*

Waiter: Oh! **Sumimasen** – *I'll fix that for you right away.*

[The waiter comes back with the cappuccino.]

Waiter: **Sumimasen** – *thank you for waiting. Here is your coffee.*

Erin: That's perfect – **sumimasen.**

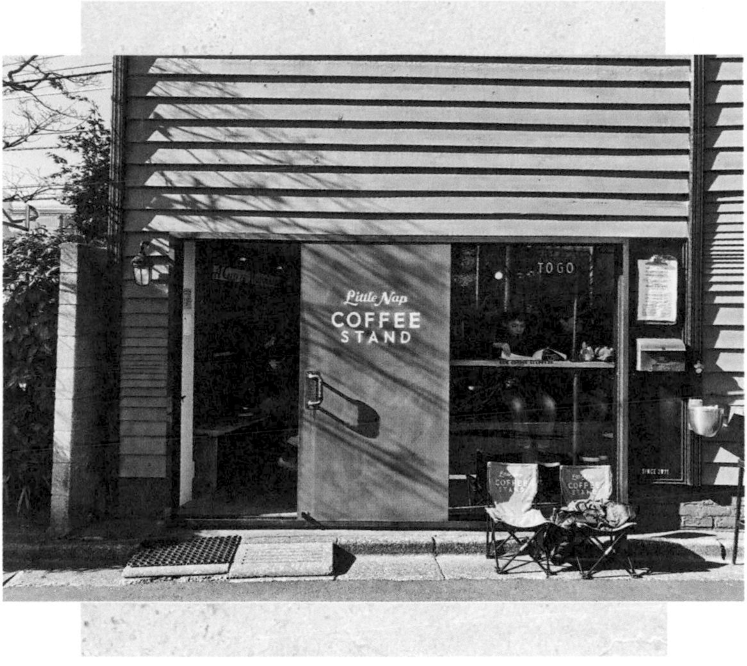
Little Nap
COFFEE
STAND
TOGO

The *Teinei* Art of Gift-giving

If you have Japanese friends, you might notice that gift-giving is something that is highly valued among them. Even if it's not your birthday, you might expect to get gifts on specific occasions. Some of these might be:

Omiyage – a gift or souvenir that you give to friends, co-workers and family when you've come back from a trip.

Ochugen – a mid-year present, usually given between 1 and 15 July, to people you might be indebted to. These might include relatives, your doctor or physician, teachers, clients or your employers.

Oseibo – the gift you might give to those you are indebted to at the end of the year, usually from early to mid-December.

Presenting gifts

Presentation is key, and wrapping your gifts in a beautiful, *teinei* way can take time. One way to wrap gifts, without being wasteful (or *mottainai*) is through the use of fabrics – *tenugui* or *furoshiki*.

Tenugui 手拭い

A *tenugui* is a thin cotton hand towel, often given as a gift. About 35 x 90 cm in size, it is plainly woven, but almost always adorned with a pattern of some kind. The multipurpose *tenugui* can be used as a washcloth or a dishcloth, but is also a popular souvenir from Japan and can be used as decoration or as a headband or sweatband.

Another way to use *tenugui* is to gift wrap bottles. It's a great way to deck out a bottle of wine (or champagne, or *sake* – whatever takes your fancy).

How to wrap a bottle

1

Lay your *tenugui* down on a surface, fold it in half and fold it in half again, so you have a faint outline of four rectangles where the folds are precise and even. Unfold the *tenugui* and lay it down flat.

2

Place your bottle down horizontally, so that the bottom of the bottle is at the centre of the *tenugui* – ideally, on the bottom right-hand side.

3

Lift the *tenugui* fabric on the side that is closest to you and roll it around the bottle. The fabric should envelop the bottle, so it looks like you have a large pipe or a sausage.

4

Making sure that the edge of the cloth is on the top of the bottle, take the fabric that is on the side nearest the mouth, and twist it around.

5

Take the fabric on the other side of the bottle (near the bottom) and lay it over the bottle. Take both ends and secure them by tying around the neck of the bottle to create a little bow – like a bowtie.

Furoshiki 風呂敷

Furoshikis ('bath spreads') were traditionally used to prevent clothing mix-ups at the bathhouses (*sento*). They were used to wrap and transport *kimonos* and were usually adorned with crests or the names of the bathers, so that they wouldn't accidentally try to pop someone else's garments on once they had finished bathing.

But *furoshiki* use spread beyond covering and transporting clothes to wrapping other objects, even more so in recent times as a response to climate change and a desire to reduce consumption of plastic and paper.

While *tenuguis* are rectangular, *furoshikis* are square. They come in various sizes and are commonly used to wrap gifts.

All you need to wrap a gift with *furoshiki* is the material itself – no tape or glue are required, meaning that you can potentially use the material again and again. Your *furoshiki* should be thick enough to withstand the weight of most gifts. You can also tie *furoshikis* and fashion them into handbags – the possibilities are endless.

Top Furoshiki tips

— **Diagonal folds are key:** in order to make sure that your gift isn't visible, make sure you fold the material over your gift diagonally, so that from an aerial view it looks like a triangle.

— **Knot a problem:** think of the *furoshiki* knot as a big bow and try to keep it on the top of an object. Try to centre it as much as possible, but for long, thin gifts that you're wrapping with a *furoshiki* cloth, you can always opt for two smaller knots, one on each end of the gift, rather than trying to hold it all in with one bigger knot in the centre.

— **Iron or steam your cloth ahead of wrapping:** you want your gift to look its best, but starting off with a wrinkled fabric will always impact the final result. Make sure you give the fabric an iron beforehand if you're reusing a *furoshiki* cloth, or steam it beforehand.

Furoshiki techniques

If you want to wrap an extensive flat object ...

If you want to wrap with two knots ...

If you want to wrap with a hidden knot ...

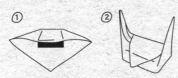

If you want to wrap two bottles of wine ...

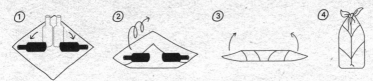

If you want to wrap with padded padding ...

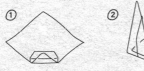

Punctuality

A lesson that really resonated with me from school was something
a teacher of mine once said, as she admonished some latecomers.
It taught me the relationship between punctuality and respect. By
consistently showing up late, she said, you believe (consciously or
not), that your time is worth more than someone else's – that they
should put their lives on hold for you, but that they don't warrant the
same from you. Others might say that those who are consistently late
are more optimistic, but tardiness is a dangerous trap to fall into
– be punctual.

Hobbies and Crafts

They say it takes two months to form a new habit or change and adapt your lifestyle in some way. If you're taking up a hobby of some kind, stick with it. One of the most encouraging feelings is when you find that you've improved at something, but nothing worth doing ever comes easily. Be *teinei* in your approach – consistently give it your all, before you give up on it. Stay accountable to yourself.

Being *teinei* is about presenting your best possible self. It goes beyond just being polite, or considerate, or thoughtful – it's about adding beauty and care to the world around you.

Practice makes perfect and being *teinei* encourages you to pay attention to the smaller details, the finer things in life. It's less about grand gestures, more about little acts of kindness. When I think of my grandfather being *teinei*, I think about the orange tree he planted in his garden the year my cousin and I were born. He spent years tending it, and because it never bore fruit, we used to joke that he was scammed when he got the seeds. It got there eventually, almost twenty years later (and after his death), but he had remained *teinei* in his approach – he never gave up, giving it the same level of care and attention, even when it was slow to produce the desired results.

Remember that this is part of a wider process – it's a marathon, not a sprint. We all have to start somewhere, and we won't get it right the first time. There is a Japanese proverb, 'A bad craftsman never made a perfect vase'. It takes time to become an expert in something, but any attempt, no matter how badly executed, is always a step in the right direction.

I'm still trying to be as *teinei* as possible, with varying degrees of success – but hey, at least I now know not to arrive at a party with a half-open packet of curry sauce.

ZAKKA

雑貨

The Beauty of Miscellaneous Things

EVERYTHING HAS BEAUTY, BUT NOT EVERYONE SEES IT.

Confucius

Zakka is a concept and design phenomenon that is really hard to put into words. While the direct translation of the word is something akin to 'miscellaneous goods', it's so much more than that. It's about finding joy and satisfaction in the seemingly commonplace or unremarkable – to find contentment and gratitude in the everyday.

Objects and clothing that are *zakka* in style are special and noteworthy because of the emotions they evoke. They are exceptional in their ordinariness – humble, mundane, everyday – yet they evoke a sense of nostalgia. They are of high quality, inexpensive and are most definitely not flashy. They illicit feelings of calm. They are not necessarily 'on trend'.

Zakka lies in contrast to heavy branding and consumerism – which, of course, are also present in Japanese culture. Objects that are *zakka* are plain, unpretentious, laden with subtext and can be ambiguous. However, they have to be useful – and there is joy in that usefulness. Pretty much anything can be *zakka* – examples include toys; household goods like pots, pans and kettles; groceries; pens; stacks of notepads; salt and pepper shakers.

There is a hint of Nordic or Scandinavian design in *zakka* – in its clarity and simplicity.

Contemporary household items can be *zakka* in that they evoke feelings of gratitude and romanticism. Items that induce nostalgia can also qualify – products and goods from the 50s, 60s and 70s are often considered to be *zakka*.

In the fashion world, comparisons can be made between *zakka* and the normcore movement. Normcore (a portmanteau of 'normal' and 'hardcore') is a trend with an emphasis on unflashy, practical and plain clothing, often casualwear. Normcore wearers consciously and deliberately choose clothing that is functional and understated. But their look isn't crudely 'thrown together', or an accident – it is curated.

Subtext: What Isn't Being Said

Part of what gives objects that are *zakka* an element of something palpable, or charm, is their subtext – what is represented or isn't being said. In order to properly understand what is *zakka*, it's important to understand the nuances in various Japanese philosophies, or ways of thinking:

— ***Mono no aware*:** the bittersweet nature of being, an acute awareness of transience, a melancholic look at mortality – a feeling of poignant appreciation and self-awareness.
— ***Wabi-sabi*:** the acceptance of, and finding the beauty in, transience and imperfection.
— ***Ma*:** often translated to mean 'negative space', the concept of *ma* can also refer to an interval, or emptiness. The word 'emptiness' might have negative connotations, but this isn't necessarily the case. *Ma*, as an aesthetic, is empty in the same way as a pause in a conversation – even when nothing is being said, things can be conveyed in the silence. The *kanji* characters for the word *ma* combine the characters for a door (門) and the sun (日) – while the gap is empty, the space it provides is infused with possibility and awareness, and allows for relationships between people, objects and things within it – which are illuminated by the emptiness of the space.

Zakka and the Importance of Making Space

Much of the appeal of *zakka* comes from its simplicity. It's not garish or flamboyant, but muted and understated. It's not distracting, allowing for space – to create and think without interruption.

How can you make space?

— Remove branding from objects.

We are constantly being sold to, whether we like it or not. On our daily commutes we are bombarded with messaging and advertisements – and as we spend a great deal of our lives on our phones and other devices, it's hard to rise above that noise. One way to lower the volume, as it were, would be to remove branding from products in your home, or consider decanting liquids or other things into plain bottles or storage containers.

— Embrace wear and tear.

This takes in the aesthetic and philosophy behind *wabi-sabi*. As things age, they might take on another hue, or get scuffed. Rather than fight against it, think about the stories and memories they evoke, and cultivate an appreciation for their new form.

— Make sure you feel good.

Zakka isn't just about collecting useful and practical things – it's about finding joy, satisfaction and happiness in using them.

— Keep it simple, stupid.

Simplicity is what makes *zakka* notable – it's not about being flashy or having the latest state-of-the-art gadget.

Ultimately, while *zakka* is a style, or an aesthetic, and revolves around objects and things, it's more about how an individual sees the spirituality in these inanimate entities. Perhaps because of the Shinto belief system and its ties with animism, *zakka* encourages us to find these qualities in the objects we curate and collect around us. It's a form of self-expression, but rather than the focus being on consumption and consumerism, it is about seeing beauty in the mundane.

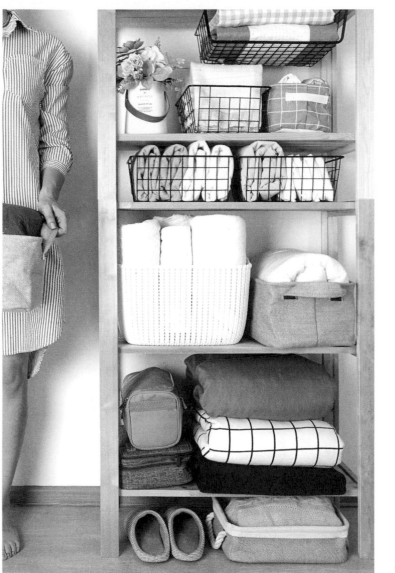

My favourite *zakka* items

— A white stovetop Le Creuset kettle

It's incredibly simple and plain, but I love the whistling sound it makes when my water is boiled. The idea that I can take it with me, anywhere in the world, and make a cup of tea with it brings me so much joy for something so routine.

— A gold watering can

I have a simple and elegant gold watering can. It's got an incredibly thin handle and spout, and using it to tend my plants always brings me contentment and satisfaction.

— A stack of 1.5mm black ballpoint pens

I enjoy a thick, strong line, so I'm particular about the pens I use. I keep them all together in a little black box. I don't get to use pens as much as I'd like to, but whenever I'm working on a project, I always put pen to paper first, before I type anything.

— A handmade ceramic teacup from Kamakura

It's muted and understated, but I feel like this cup was made for me – it fits so perfectly into the palm of my hand. It's beige, with little black and grey flecks from the glaze.

Part 2:

Omoiyari

思いやり

FORTUNE WILL ALWAYS COME INTO A HOUSE WITH LAUGHTER.

Japanese proverb

Omoiyari is often translated to mean empathy, but it's more than that. It's about pre-emptively thinking about what might make someone happy, or more comfortable, more at ease.

Over the course of writing this book, I had the pleasure of hearing stories and examples of people's experiences of *omoiyari* in Japan. One was from someone who had spent their summer in Yokohama as part of an exchange programme. They had been staying with a family, in a three-room apartment. During their time there, the parents of the house gave up their bedroom for their guest, the mother and daughter sharing a room, while the father slept on a *futon* under the kitchen table.

Another story, from friends who were in Japan for the Rugby World Cup, concerned a stranger who overheard them speaking English and took them on a tour of various *izakayas* (Japanese-style bars), paying for their drinks, telling them, 'I'm not a wealthy man, but tonight I'm rich'.

In many instances, the stories of kindness that resonated with people the most involved strangers. All the relationships were, in some sense, fleeting – a guest for a week, a drinking buddy for the evening. These are all examples of individuals extending the feeling of *omoiyari* to others – through kindness and hospitality. But when you are on the receiving end, the result is anything but fleeting – it stays with you.

Omoiyari is a form of altruistic sensitivity. It is about compassion – almost curating an experience for others, based on anticipating their needs in advance and preparing accordingly, putting a plan in place. It goes beyond the self. Consideration for others, and relationships are at the heart of *omoiyari*.

In order to properly explain *omoiyari*, I wanted to concentrate on concepts and activities relating to building and cultivating relationships with others. So the second part of this book focuses on the concepts of *wa* (harmony) and *onkochishin* (respecting the past), and practical, actionable ways in which you can demonstrate your fondness for others – through the art of creating *senbazuru* (a thousand paper cranes), or *omakase* (placing your faith in a stranger) and experiencing the joy of eating together and sharing food. *Omoiyari* as a concept also comes through with the idea of *omotenashi* – the art of selfless hospitality.

Practising *omoiyari*, and embodying it in your day-to-day life, requires faith in others. This means you have to be a bit of an optimist and be open to vulnerability – to seek the good in other people and believe that they will have your best interests at heart. It won't always work out – the palate of a chef preparing an *omakase* meal for you, for example, might be altogether different from yours. But the rewards from taking the risks make it worth cherishing, and worthy of appreciation.

I think we need to be more compassionate, and practise demonstrating it more in our daily lives. In many ways, there are more divisions than ever before – we live in chaotic and turbulent times. But I believe that we can overcome the challenges and obstacles we face; in many ways, I am a prime example of this.

As I mentioned earlier, as the daughter of a Japanese mother and a British father, I had four grandparents who all lived through the Second World War. Nothing compares to the horrors of warfare, and they all grew up in a time of scarcity, and of fear. For my great-grandfather (the father of my English grandmother, Gilly), the thought of his grandson bringing home a Japanese girlfriend from university must have stirred up an extremely difficult and challenging set of

emotions and memories. Prior to their meeting, his understanding of Japanese people would have been based on wartime narratives, and his perceptions of them would have come from a place of prejudice. But this changed when he actually met my mother, Eriko – and they had a wonderful relationship. Although he died when I was very young, I remember him as a warm, extremely loving presence. I've been incredibly lucky that for most of my life my grandparents (who were not, of course, immune to the usual family politics) have had the utmost respect, affection and feelings of kindness towards each other. And it's because of this that I am a true believer in the power of *omoiyari* and, more widely, respect and compassion. *Omoiyari* is graceful, thoughtful and selfless; it's about the generosity of kindness – something that we can all aspire to.

05

WA

和

Harmony

DIFFERENT BODY, SAME MIND.

Japanese proverb

Of all the concepts I've covered so far, *wa* might be the most challenging to distill. *Wa* represents harmony, peace, balance and unity and comes through a multitude of traditions, practices and platforms. It is perhaps so tricky to nail down because it permeates all aspects of Japanese culture. In fact, *wa* is also a name for Japan, or Japanese things – a *washitsu* is a Japanese-style room with *tatami* floors; *washi* paper is Japanese paper; *washoku* is Japanese food; *wafuku* is Japanese clothing, like *kimonos*; and anything Japanese-style is referred to as *wafu*.

The philosophy of *wa* is one of harmonious cohesion, focusing on the needs of the community, rather than more self-serving, individual interests. It's a celebration of the interconnectedness of things, and their relationships, as opposed to seeing things in isolation. Whether it is tea ceremony, *shinrin-yoku* (forest bathing), cherry-blossom season or *Bushido* (the way of the warrior), the concept of *wa* flows through it all.

The idea of *wa* not only refers to the interconnectedness or connection between people, but between people and physical objects, too. It is based on the belief that objects are imbued with a kind of spiritual power. *Wa* is about the pursuit of balance – finding harmony among people, the space in which they reside and how they are connected and the interplay between all these factors.

In Harmony with Nature

Many traditional Japanese practices and pastimes are focused on the attainment of tranquillity, or this sense of harmony – the pursuit of *wa*, particularly maintaining a close relationship with the natural world.

Shinrin-yoku: forest bathing

Shinrin-yoku is a therapeutic practice, which involves becoming immersed in nature and awakening our senses. It is about connecting with the environment mindfully, and without premeditation – more of a ramble than a jog.

Many studies have shown that this practice has tangible benefits – from improving cardiovascular health to aiding sleep. I firmly believe that anyone can benefit from *shinrin-yoku*, even those who live in an urban environment. There's something about the stillness that being immersed in nature can bring – the combination of physical activity and mental clarity is extremely valuable.

Here are a few tips for practising *shinrin-yoku* in the city:

— Leave your devices at home – this is about shutting out noise and being present in the moment.

— Look out for natural phenomena around you – things like *komorebi* (the light that filters through leaves), *kawaakari* (see below) or moss growing in a particular way. What season is it? How are the trees changing? These are the details that will reveal themselves to you on your journey.

— Avoid following a set path. This is about letting your mind wander freely, and letting go, rather than following strict guidelines or sticking to a prescribed timeframe.

Hanami: enjoying the transient beauty of flowers

Hanami is the tradition of viewing flowers, particularly between March and May during the cherry-blossom season. People take advantage of this transient and beautiful phenomenon by gathering for parties in the parks. Any excuse for a get-together with good food and *sake*!

Kawaakari: the light of a river in darkness

The term '*kawaakari*' refers to the soft light or glow of a river's surface in darkness, often caused by the reflection of the moon on the water. This is just one example of the phenomena you might encounter when you practise *kachou fuugetsu* – getting to know yourself through experiencing the beauty and majesty of the natural world.

Chado: Tea Ceremony

Chado, or 'the way of tea', is the ceremonial presentation of tea, through a series of prescribed movements that are meticulously thought out, planned and executed.

Like many Japanese practices, it is never just about the tea – it's also about the food, decorative elements (like *ikebana* flower arrangements, the display of calligraphy, selection of ceramics) and clothing, too. It is a constantly fluid and changing process, one in which the practitioner takes into account the passage of time and changing of the seasons. My aunt, for example, has devoted years (in fact, decades) to honing her craft.

The principles of tea ceremony include:

— *Wa* – **harmony in nature** In the context of tea ceremony, it is about how the elements of the practice relate to the outside world, but also how the selection of food, ceramics and other details relate to the space, and to the manner in which it is served to the guests.

— *Kei* – **respect** In tea ceremony, it is about respecting each other, but also the objects and the process itself.

— *Sei* – **purity** Finding clarity and stillness of mind, the act of tea ceremony itself is a purification of sorts.

— *Jaku* – **tranquillity** The aim is to find and embody tranquillity through the art of tea ceremony.

In order to properly understand *wa*, practising tea ceremony, or a version of it, might bring a sense of awareness, and help to change your perception.

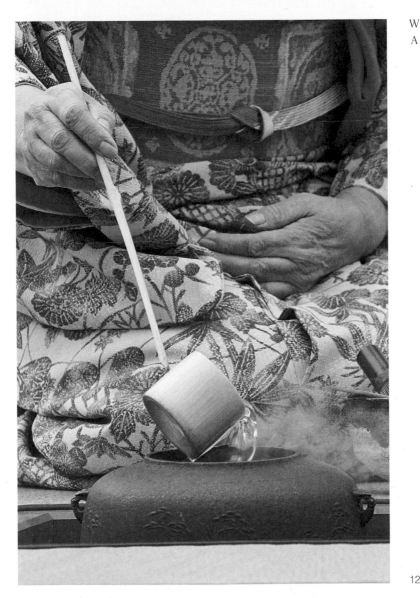

How to Host a Tea Ceremony in Six Steps

By following these six simple steps, you can bring the practice of tea ceremony, with all its benefits, into your home and life.

1. **Prepare the space.** Whether you're doing it at home, or elsewhere, you need to prepare the space. Make sure it's clean and, ideally, includes a scenic view or elements of nature.
2. **Prepare the guests.** Ahead of the tea ceremony, you want to make your guests feel welcome, and put them at ease. The joy and benefit of *chado*, particularly tranquillity, are all about leaving the daily concerns and worries aside for the duration of the ceremony.
3. **Prepare the tools.** What flowers are on display? What items will you be serving, and what will you be serving them in? Make sure you have these to hand and are not scrambling around looking for things in front of guests. In tea ceremony, the transitions between courses and stages are seamless – the act of popping the kettle on is one that is carefully choreographed.
4. **Prepare the tea.** The most important part of tea ceremony is the tea itself – make sure it's not too bitter. Why not try matcha tea?
5. **Serve the tea.** In traditional tea ceremony, all guests would drink from the same teacup, which is ceremonially wiped and cleaned before being handed to the next guest. If you're having a tea ceremony at home, consider serving tea in a way that encourages communal engagement – cutting slices from one cake, for example, rather than serving individual slices ahead of time.
6. **Clean up.** Purity is one of the tenets of the practice – always be thinking of the next tea ceremony, and clear your area in a way that isn't creating work for the next person (or for yourself in the future).

Bushido: The Way of the Warrior

My great-great-grandmother was from a *samurai* family based in Mie Prefecture. The word *samurai* roughly translates to 'one that serves', but it has come to mean warrior. In reality, *samurai* were those of noble birth who were armed supporters of wealthy landowners. The closest parallel to *Bushido* might be the concept of chivalry – a medieval code of conduct of sorts.

While their roles evolved and changed over the course of hundreds of years, there are eight core virtues of *Bushido* that provide valuable insight and a useful framework even for us today:

— Justice (*gi*)

Perhaps the most important virtue is that of justice – acting with integrity and honesty. This has as much to do with yourself as your dealings with others: are you ready to stand by your decisions? Are you willing to be open to accepting a view, despite your personal feelings?

— Courage (*yu*)

Taking risks, and being brave – doing what is right, even if it scares you.

— Compassion (*jin*)

As warriors, *samurai* wielded a great deal of power and responsibility, with the ability to enforce punishment, command and even kill. As part of the *Bushido* code, or the Way of the *Samurai*, it was important to be able to demonstrate compassion, mercy and benevolence.

— Respect (*rei*)

Those who lived by the *Bushido* code were expected to conduct themselves in a certain manner, demonstrating respect, politeness and good manners. In many ways, full of grace.

— Honesty (*makoto*)

Honesty and sincerity, trustworthiness.

— Honour (*meiyo*)

A sense of dignity, pride, particularly in relation to their work – putting their best selves forward and holding themselves up to the highest standards.

— Loyalty (*chūgi*)

The *samurai* were accountable and responsible for their own actions, as well as those in their care, and had to demonstrate a sense of loyalty.

— Character (*jisei*)

In order to keep their titles the *samurai* had to demonstrate strength and moral character. Self-control, valour and willpower were essential virtues for those who lived by the *Bushido* code.

AMONG BLOSSOMS, THE CHERRY BLOSSOM; AMONG MEN, THE WARRIOR.

Japanese proverb

Bringing the Principles of *Wa* into Your Life

Many traditional Japanese practices are deeply tied to the concept and the principles of *wa*, yet it is possible to bring these into your everyday life, too. And I believe that by embracing the *wa* in your life you can bring harmony and contentment, as well as clarity of mind, in many ways.

Less is more

If *wa* is about the interconnectedness of relationships, then we need the space to be able to truly see these relationships for what they are – away from the noise of it all; away from waste, and the pursuit of the 'next big thing'. Take a moment to examine what you have. Take your time. There is a proverb – *ichinichiippo*, meaning one day, one step. Don't rush your decisions, but chip away at a big task slowly. As they say, the deepest rivers run slowly.

Let go of perfection and symmetry

Perfection is a myth, as is the concept of symmetry. Embrace the concept of *wabi-sabi* – the idea of impermanence, transience and imperfection. Find the beauty in the stories that the cracks and frays reveal.

Respect each other

The concept of *wa* is intrinsically linked with ideas of group unity, cohesion and, ultimately, happiness. None of this is possible without respect. So act with compassion and respect for others, even if they aren't capable of showing it themselves.

Reiwa – the New Era

When writing about various philosophies or concepts, it can be easy to second guess yourself about your understanding of it. Is the concept of *wa* even relevant in this day and age? Is it important? A new era – the *Reiwa* era (meaning 'beautiful harmony') – began on 1 May 2019, as Emperor Naruhito succeeded his father, following his abdication due to old age and declining health. The naming of each era is done with a great deal of thought, and by a council of experts. It is customary to have one era per Emperor, and to rename the Emperor using the name of the era over which he presided – for example, Hirohito was given the posthumous name of *Showa Tenno,* after the Showa era.

This book will have been published during the second year of the *Reiwa* period – and the idea of a beautiful, harmonious and Japanese society was significant in naming it.

Since I wrote my first book, there have been a great many changes in the world, but two in particular seem significant here, and luckily, they coincide: the birth of my first niece during the first year of the *Reiwa* period. For many, the name represents 'a culture being born and nurtured by people coming together, beautifully'.[3] For me, it signifies the hope for a harmonious, bright and peaceful future.

In my opinion, the art of *omoiyari* – compassion, and acting in a thoughtful way towards others – grows out of *wa*. The desire for harmony, or the culture of maintaining these ideals and balance, naturally lends itself to acting in a way that benefits not only yourself, but a wider group.

Omoiyari isn't just about how you treat others, but also the world around you, and yourself. In order to truly understand and appreciate *wa*, it's important to pause and reflect. Where are you physically, in a specific moment in time? Where are you spiritually or emotionally? How does this fit into the larger picture of the life you want to live, and to leave behind? These are big questions – and sometimes, it's nice to think about them over a cup of tea.

OMOTENASHI

おもてなし

The Art of Selfless Hospitality

Because life is full of uncertainty, one must engrave in his heart the events of the day as if there were no tomorrow.

Today's tea ceremony is a once-in-a-lifetime experience, and one, along with his guests, must wholeheartedly approach the meeting with sincerity.

Sen no Rikyu, the great *chado* master

Whenever I speak to anyone who has been to Japan, I'm always regaled with stories of what they enjoyed – the incredible food, the beautiful scenery, the stunning shrines. But what I love hearing about most is the kindness they've noticed through interactions with the people there – stories of *omotenashi*.

Omotenashi describes the spirit of Japanese hospitality. The word, a combination of *omote* (public face) and *nashi* (nothing, or without), perfectly encapsulates the approach Japanese people take to the concept of hospitality – doing things for others, without the expectation of anything in return.

In the process of writing this book, I reached out to see if people would share their experiences with me:

'On one occasion, I started speaking to people at the neighbouring table at a restaurant. After a pleasant conversation, they ended up paying for my meal, without expecting anything in return. I was really surprised, and told them it wasn't necessary, but they insisted. My Japanese friends told me it's not uncommon, and a way to be hospitable to friendly strangers.'

'My husband and I spent a week in Ishigaki Island. One day, we decided to go a different route, and couldn't find the beach. We finally found a bus stop and noticed that the next bus was coming in forty-five minutes. My husband had spoken to a local couple who had driven past earlier in a car. They drove by the bus stop, and offered to take us to the next hotspot, driving half an hour out of their way to do so.'

'When we were in Japan and on the train for the first time, there was a lovely man who talked to us and realised it was our first day (when we were in the station buying our tickets). We got a bit lost, and he got on the train with us and took us to our stop, even though he wasn't going that way.'

'In this tiny public bathhouse where we went for lunch, the one English-speaking member of staff asked where were going next. We said we wanted to stop off at a local doughnut shop, then go to the station. She relayed this to the manager, he looked at his watch, shrugged and next thing we knew we were getting dropped off by him – he even waited for us to get our doughnuts.'

'After an epic dinner with my work colleagues, I accidentally dropped my slim camera through the small gap of the elevator shaft, and quickly realised it would be completely smashed, given that the bar was located on the top floor of the hotel. It was about 12am, and I was meant to be flying back the following day. I went straight to reception to ask if it was possible for someone to check if the memory stick could be located in the coming days. I had taken so many pictures and videos of our trip and didn't want to lose them. The receptionist seemed even more sad than I was at the thought of losing these memories. Next thing I knew, around 7am, an envelope was slipped through my door. It contained various small pieces of my camera, and a note to say that while they hadn't found the memory stick, they would keep looking. Around two weeks later, I received a package in London containing the remaining camera pieces, along with the memory stick.'

What really strikes me about these stories is that they are not isolated incidents. This doesn't make them any less special, but tales of kindness, consideration and going above and beyond for others (often complete strangers), with no expectation of payment (in Japan, tipping isn't customary) or getting anything back in return are not uncommon.

You will find examples of *omotenashi* not only in interactions between people, but in the way various experiences are planned out as well. At a restaurant, for example, you might notice little details that make the process run more smoothly – a hot towel on arrival, for

instance, or the fact that you are able to see what you order before it arrives, from a display of carefully crafted sample models of dishes. Both the hot towel and the displays have been prepared wholly for the guests' benefit; but this conscientious approach extends beyond dining out – from taking a taxi (doors that open and close automatically) to cleaners on the bullet train bowing to the train in respect as it arrives in the station. The needs of others are anticipated in advance, and small details are catered and planned for.

Omotenashi differs from customer service in the sense that it isn't based on a hierarchy – it is not about doing something because it's part of a job. *Omotenashi* has roots in *chado* tea ceremony and, as a result, is more about respect and harmony than serving another person. *Ichi-go ichi-e* – a phrase also associated with tea ceremony – describes the fleeting and transient nature of an instant. It highlights the need to cherish each moment, as if it were the only one you will experience in your lifetime. The lesson to be learned here? Treat everyone, and every moment, like it is something precious and important, because it can't be repeated.

ICHI-GO
ICHI-E
一期一会
ONE TIME,
ONE
MEETING.

Treasuring every moment, as it cannot be repeated.

The *Omotenashi* Dictionary

As I write about *omotenashi*, a couple of other terms spring to mind that might be useful in helping you to consider your approach to interacting with others, whether in a personal or professional capacity.

Sumimasen すみません

We came across *sumimasen* earlier (see p.82), meaning 'excuse me', 'thank you' or 'I'm sorry'. But where it relates to *omotenashi*, or doing things without the expectation of anything in return, *sumimasen* can be about how people can work together. In the context of a shop, for example, you might hear the word used when staff change over during a shift, or lend a hand to colleagues who might need help with a specific task. It's about showing respect for the effort of your colleagues, and working to lighten their load, too.

Genki 元気

Whenever I switch over to the Japanese keyboard on my mobile to text someone, the phone always automatically predicts that I'll type in '*genki*' – perhaps the most common question I pose to people, asking whether or not they are *genki*. *Genki* translates to mean healthy, lively, energetic – to be cheerful and in good spirits. It can also be described as a force that permeates life – a good energy. You can notice the spirit of *genki* in others, and people will try to approach their interactions with others in a *genki* way.

Kokoroire 心入れ

In Japanese, there are three words for the heart. One is *shinzou*, which refers to the organ that pumps blood around the body. The second is *ha-to*, which refers to the shape of a love heart. The third is *kokoro*, which means the heart, mind and spirit – these are all interlinked within the term. In Japanese tea ceremony, you might do things in a *kokoroire* manner, meaning that everything you do when you perform tea ceremony is done with heartfelt devotion. You put your heart into it and give it your all.

Omotenashi in Practice

Acting in a way that demonstrates the intent of *omotenashi*, the art of selfless hospitality, or putting the needs of others before your own, might feel challenging. Here are a few ways to approach it.

Anticipating needs

One of the reasons why the *omotenashi* approach is so remarkable is that your needs, or the needs of others, are predicted and anticipated in advance, and are prepared for accordingly. Things might appear, seemingly as if by magic, but they have been carefully and meticulously planned out ahead of time, to ensure your comfort and enjoyment. You can do this by taking a human-centred approach to your planning. Put yourself in the shoes of others – what might make them happy, or make an experience more enjoyable for them?

Selflessness

It's natural and human to crave praise and reassurance, but *omotenashi* isn't about getting personal or individual attention – that would make it a selfish act.

Do things for others without needing the credit. Think less about your own individual impulses, and more about what you can do to make your environment better – helping to make the world more harmonious by demonstrating and embodying kindness.

Recognising it in others

Omotenashi is about respect. Think about a tea ceremony – yes, there is a host, but the guests play an integral part in the practice, and the beauty of it comes from respect and balance. Try to seek out the positive in others; remember to thank them – and even if they insist on not wanting repayment, take inspiration from them and pay it back in other ways.

It's also important not to take advantage of the kindness of others. If someone has a generous spirit, it can be easy to rely on them – but remember that they have limits, and that you need to know yours, too.

Paying it forward

If you have been on the receiving end of an act of kindness, try to pay it forward. It can be something as small as buying a coffee for the next person in line – but remember those little acts can have an incredible impact.

THOUGH WE
MEET BUT
ONCE, EVEN
BY CHANCE,
WE ARE
FRIENDS
FOR LIFE.

Okinawan saying

There is a Japanese idiom, *fugen jikkō*, a combination of four kanji characters that translates to meaning 'actions over words'. The expression perfectly captures the spirit behind *omotenashi* – to act in a way that the individual in question might want for nothing. The selfless nature of *omotenashi*, without any expectation of reward or return, is at the heart of *omoiyari*. They are closely intertwined, and in many ways you are not able to have one without the other.

In order to behave in a compassionate manner (with *omoiyari*) you must be selfless, and to conduct yourself in a way that might not seem immediately advantageous (*omotenashi*). The beauty and the benefit that both can provide is subtle – it has soft power. Just like the sensation you get when you see a loved one take a bite of a meal you've spent a long time preparing, or when they open a special gift you've chosen for them, there is so much joy to be experienced by doing things for others. The feeling of excitement, happiness and contentment that you experience when you help others is infectious. I believe it is this feeling that we're chasing when we behave in this way – we want to tap into that emotion in a way that is deeper and more meaningful than if we were doing it just for ourselves.

07

ONKOCHISHIN

温故知新

Learning from the Past

ONKOCHISHIN

RETAINING THE PAST TO UNDERSTAND THE FUTURE.

Japanese proverb

The Japanese phrase *onkochishin* means to gain new understanding through revising what has been learned. This is about reflecting on the past, and using that as a framework to understand your present and consider what new changes you can bring about as a result.

The most significant part isn't about looking back – this isn't about ruminating in an obsessive manner over things you can't change. (Perhaps the proverb 'Let the past drift away with the water' might bring you more comfort in these cases.) No, the sentiment behind *onkochishin* is one that inspires action. The last character of the phrase – 新 – stands for 'new'. It's about what the lessons learned can bring to your future, and the changes and insights that reveal themselves to you in the process. How can you learn from the past to understand your future?

One of the first times I properly and deliberately reflected upon the Japanese cultural approach to things was during my time at university. As an anthropology student, the module I struggled with the most was the one about Japan. I'd naively assumed that it would be a breeze, freeing up my afternoons, so I could focus on some of the subjects I found a bit more challenging. That was my first mistake.

At the moment of victory, tighten the straps of your helmet.

Tokugawa Ieyasu, founder and first shogun of the Tokugawa shogunate of Japan

The lessons I learned during that module would turn out to be some of the most valuable of my entire university experience. For the first time, I was forced to think and reflect upon my own culture objectively. I grew to enjoy it, and write about it, which eventually led to my first book.

Another thing I reflected upon in greater detail through that course was the concept of *kaizen* – perhaps responsible for the rapid strides in Japanese manufacturing following the Second World War. *Kaizen*, or 'good change', refers to a concept whereby small, incremental changes take place, leading to continuous improvement in systems and processes. *Kaizen* is only effective due to the fact that ongoing reflection is built into the workflow. By understanding what might not have worked previously, you continue to move forward.

More generally, for me, *kaizen* is linked to the idea of learning and reflecting on what has come before. It's not possible to evolve and improve without understanding this – and how it informs the way we approach whatever comes next.

Festivals, Rituals and Celebrations

So *onkochishin* is about respecting the past, while looking forward to the future. Various rituals and celebrations throughout the course of the year really highlight this idea, in that they give you time to remember, reflect and reminisce – but they also give you hope and excitement for what is yet to come.

Shichi-Go-San 七五三

As I mentioned earlier, I recently became an aunt, and one of the things I'm really looking forward to is celebrating my niece's *Shichi-Go-San* when she is three years old, and again when she is seven. *Shichi-Go-San* is a custom observed around 15 November, when girls of three and seven years of age (and boys aged five) dress in traditional cothing and go to visit a shrine to celebrate a rite of passage. They are given *chitose ame* ('thousand-year candy'), which symbolises healthy growth and longevity.

The tradition started in the seventh century, when, due to the high rate of infant mortality, children were not officially registered until they were three years old. But while the origins of the festival might be administrative in nature, nowadays it is cause for celebration. At three, five and seven, children begin to show different stages of development – and the *Shichi-Go-San* observes this.

For many parents, celebrating with their children through this age-old tradition reminds them of their own milestones, giving them not only an opportunity to reflect, but also a sense of excitement about their children's future.

Coming of Age Day 成人の日

Seijin no hi, or Coming of Age Day, is a holiday held on the second Monday of January, to celebrate those who have come of age (or turned twenty) between 2 April the previous year and 1 April in the current year.

People celebrate by wearing traditional dress, and they receive small gifts following the ceremony, which is typically held at city-hall ward offices. Usually a visit to a shrine takes place before the obligatory after-parties start, as those who have come of age start to exercise their new rights and privileges!

Respect for the Aged Day 敬老の日

The spirit of *omoiyari,* or compassion, comes from a place of respect and consideration for others. Particularly given the rapidly ageing population of Japan, many aspects of Japanese society and culture are designed around inclusivity, involving the elderly.

Respect for the Aged Day takes place on the third Monday of September, as a national holiday, to honour and celebrate senior citizens. As well as the news and media covering stories around some of the oldest members of the population in Japan, people also take the time to return home and visit their older relatives or perhaps to volunteer with those in their community. Children and younger people might also put on shows and entertainment for them as well.

Respect for the Aged Day is about what the different generations can learn from each other, and it's also about reducing isolation for older people, as well as fostering inter-generational relationships. One of my favourite and most vivid childhood memories is of the time my grandmother (who I call *Baba)* came to my kindergarten with all the other grandmothers, and my classmates and I were tasked with making a cream stew for them.

Obon お盆

Many cultures have festivals and celebrations to honour the spirits of their ancestors and relatives. *Obon*, sometimes referred to as just *Bon*, is the Japanese version.

Obon is a time for family reunions, for paying your respects to those who have departed and for welcoming the spirits back home temporarily. People visit and clean the graves of their ancestors, as well as their household altars. The date varies, depending on where in Japan you are, but it always takes place in the summer when, due to the heat, people will usually wear cotton *kimonos* called *yukata*, as they are light and breathable.

Obon festivals feature a traditional dance (a '*Bon Odori*'), to welcome back the spirits of the dead. There are also often carnivals with rides, games and food stands. The *Obon* festival closes with a bonfire, to send the spirits back home. The dead are transported back to the spirit world through a *toro nagashi*, whereby paper lanterns are floated across a river to guide their souls home.

Onkochishin: How to Create
New Beginnings From Old Patterns

What can we learn from *onkochishin*? How can we forge new ideas from the old ways?

Change things up

It can be easy to stick to a routine and stay where you are comfortable, but try to incorporate different activities into your day-to-day. Why not try a different sport, instead of just hitting the gym, or add a new colour to your wardrobe? Think about what's worked for you in the past, as well as old habits that no longer serve you, and try something new and a little exciting instead – don't stick to what's 'normal'.

Create space for reflection

I write a gratitude journal every day. Just a list of three things I'm grateful for, or that have made me smile. These may be incredibly small, but it means that I take the time, every day, to pause and reflect on the day I've had, and on the positive. Some days are a lot harder than others, but creating time to reflect allows me the mental clarity not to repeat things that I don't enjoy. In the same way that the *Shichi-Go-San* celebrations make us find the time to mark specific milestones, it's important to find time for this activity. I also try, every so often, to read back and remember the small details from the previous months. Days are long, but years are short – they can so easily go by unnoticed, and the tiniest details can bring you happiness and contentment. Take the time to celebrate them.

Seek the perspectives of others

Some of the most valuable advice I've received has been from those older than me, or those with whom it might seem, on the surface, that I have little in common. Try to surround yourself with the voices and perspectives of people who don't have the same point of view as you – say, people who are older or from a completely different background. If you don't have anyone like that in your life, consider volunteering in your community – you might be surprised by who you meet.

Think kaizen

This isn't about crash diets or cramming the night before an exam. *Kaizen* is about making tiny changes and working at them over a long period of time in order to make them stick. The *kaizen* approach looks back at processes, recognising inefficiencies and things that might be a hindrance to your success, and working to provide solutions. If you're finding it hard to break a specific habit, think of it as part of a larger learning process. As the old proverb goes – 'Perseverance is strength'.

A valuable lesson that *onkochishin* can bring is that we aren't defined by our past. Sometimes, the path not taken, or a perceived misstep or missed opportunity or potential, can lead us to fear – they can be paralysing, debilitating. But it's also important not to ignore things, as if they never happened, and shut it all away.

Onkochishin is about embracing the past – the good, the bad and the ugly – and moving forwards to create something new. It's about finding appreciation for the lessons learned along the way and bringing those new perspectives with you into the next stage of your journey.

THE CRANE FOR A THOUSAND YEARS, THE TORTOISE FOR TEN THOUSAND YEARS.

Japanese proverb

08

SENBAZURU

千羽鶴

One Thousand Paper Cranes

Tsuru, or the Japanese crane, is revered not only as a symbol of peace, but also one of longevity, loyalty, fidelity and dedication.

Origami is the Japanese art of paper folding – transforming a sheet of paper into a three-dimensional creation through a few carefully placed tucks and creases. And *senbazuru* is the practice of creating a thousand paper cranes – twenty-five strings, each with a collection of forty *orizuru*, or folded paper cranes. They are given as gifts at times of celebration, like weddings, but also in the face of adversity or hardship – for example, to wish good health and a long and happy life to someone who is going through a period of illness. So creating a *senbazuru* isn't just about crafting – it's about loyalty, dedication, positive manifestation, peace and hope.

We live in an age where it is near impossible to avoid consuming content of some kind – you can get all the books you want with next-day delivery, or binge-watch an entire series over the course of a couple of days. At big sporting matches, or weddings, or exam periods, however, these *senbazuru* formations of a thousand paper *origami* cranes are still presented. Technologies change, but the feelings that the *origami* cranes evoke are eternal. Even if the paper disintegrates, and each crane is recycled or folded away, the memories of that go with them, and the well-wishes of those who are thinking of you will remain.

Longevity

In folklore, the *tsuru* is said to live for a thousand years. According to the World Health Organization, Japan is a world leader in terms of longevity and life expectancy.[4] Much of this can be attributed to a combination of genetics and diet, as well as the cultural significance placed on *ikigai*, or purpose – the idea that we should cultivate in our lives a sense of meaning derived not only from our work, but what we are good at, what the world needs and what makes us happy.

Loyalty

The presentation of a thousand paper cranes as a gift can be considered the physical manifestation of loyalty – a token of devotion and appreciation.

Fidelity

Cranes mate for life, so you will often find them as a decorative feature at marriage ceremonies – a symbol of good luck for a happy and prosperous relationship. Because cranes are monogamous, they also appear as patterns in traditional clothing, such as wedding attire. *Senbazuru* are gifted at weddings to the newlyweds to represent good fortune.

Dedication

According to legend, the act of folding a thousand paper cranes is said to grant a wish, or happiness and eternal good luck. Based on this, it is believed that the thousand *orizuru* must be completed by the same person, within the space of a year. The act of creating a *senbazuru* is a demonstration of dedication and loyalty in itself. It comes from the belief that good luck and good fortune aren't bestowed, but created; the act of patient and loyal dedication, while demonstrating commitment through attempting to replicate the beauty of the crane, will bring the creator good fortune.

I think there is an important message to be derived from the philosophy behind *senbazuru* about making your own luck. The creation of a single paper crane on its own might not have an impact or significance – but over a long period of time, your actions can have an incredible impact.

無阿弥陀佛 浄土宗 寺庭婦人会

The Power of Words: Positive Incantations

If the act of creating *senbazuru* is representative of the Japanese approach to *making* your own luck, then *engi naoshi* is all about *changing* your luck through positive incantations, or 'omen fixing'.

There is a belief that there is spiritual power (*kotodama*) behind specific words, and this is not to be wielded lightly. (*Tsurukame* – crane and turtle – is one example, the principle being that by repeating the names of two auspicious animals, over and over, you will be able to ward off evil.) It is perhaps because of this that much of Japanese culture is inferred through practices and actions. There are some words that are considered to be taboo, or *imikotoba*, and they are not used in specific contexts because of their spiritual power – they are laden with bad luck.

The lesson to be learned from *kotodama*, and *imikotoba*, is that words carry significant power and a degree of responsibility. Things that are said, even to yourself, are absorbed, and don't go into a vacuum; this is tied to a belief in the power of language to manifest into reality. Whether or not you believe in this, it's hard to deny that words hold meaning, and have power. Use them wisely, and with compassion and kindness – even if it is just for yourself.

BETTER THE ONE CRY OF A CRANE THAN A THOUSAND CHIRPS FROM SPARROWS

Japanese proverb

The Story of Sadako Sasaki

The practice of *senbazuru* is often spoken of in relation to one person in particular – a young girl named Sadako Sasaki. At two years old, Sadako became a *hibakusha* – a person affected by the atomic bombing of Hiroshima. While Sadako survived the bombing, she was severely irradiated, and died at the age of twelve from leukaemia caused by the after-effects.

Before she died, Sadako set herself the task of folding a thousand paper cranes. As paper was in short supply at the time, she made use of scrap paper – anything she could get her hands on in the hospital in an attempt to complete her objective. Some versions of the tale say she didn't make her final goal, and that her friends and family contributed to it after her death, while others say she both met and surpassed it. Either way, she became a symbol of optimism and resilience in the face of adversity. Her story became synonymous with the innocent victims of war, and her pursuit of *senbazuru* brought a message of hope and peace.

The Art of *Origami*

Origami ('*ori*' – folding or weaving; '*gami*' – paper) refers to the practice of transforming a sheet of paper into a three-dimensional work of art, using folding and sculpting methods, and without the use of glue or tape or marking.

Origami paper is square-shaped, although in more recent times materials other than paper have also been used, the only prerequisite being that the material is able to hold a crease. There are many types of origami, including:

— **action *origami*:** these have the potential to be 'animated' once in their final form – including jumping frogs, fortune tellers, aeroplanes

— **modular *origami*:** this involves combining a lot of separate identical parts to form a larger object; a *kusudama* is a popular example, in which very small *origami* flowers are sewn together to make a ball or spherical shape

— **kirigami:** a type of *origami* that *does* require cutting, but typically not the use of glue to form the final structure.

How to Create a Paper Crane (*Orizuru*)

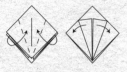

1.

Have the *origami* paper facing you on a flat surface, with one corner at the top, so it looks like the shape of a diamond. If the paper is patterned, have the patterned side facing down.

2.

Fold the paper diagonally across, so that the top corner touches the bottom corner – once folded, the paper should be in a triangle.

3.

Fold this shape in half again – it should still be a triangle, only smaller.

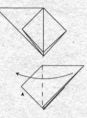

4.

At this point, the small triangle will have two 'flaps' – gently open each side, and press these down, so that each 'flap' resembles two small diamond shapes.

5.

Take the outer edges of each diamond and fold them inwards, so they resemble lapels on a jacket. These creases make the following steps easier, so make sure you unfold them before continuing.

6.

Take the top of that diamond shape, and fold it downwards, just above the other folds you have just made. Unfold this again.

7.

Next, you create the 'petal fold'. Lift the bottom corner upwards, prising the paper open. At this point, it should almost resemble a Venus flytrap. Push the two outer edges inwards, closing the paper again – it will now be longer and thinner than before.

8.

Create a petal fold on the other side, so the entire piece looks symmetrical Now, the entire piece of paper should be a very thin diamond shape.

9.

With this thinner diamond shape, make another 'lapel' fold, folding the outer corners inward. Repeat this on the other side.

10.

At this stage, you will have a very thin diamond shape with two 'legs' – these will form the tail and the beak of your crane.

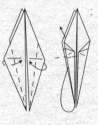

11.

Take the 'leg' on the right-hand side, and fold this gently to the right.

12.

Take the 'leg' on the left side, and fold it gently to the left, before unfolding both legs.

13.

Fold the two 'legs', so that they are inside the creases of the model and flatten everything. It should look like you have two spikes pointing upwards, on either side of the main body.

14.

Take one of these legs, and crease it gently, so it looks like a beak.

15.

In order to reveal its final form – the crane – gently pull each of the wings away from each other. This will create space in the body, and the *origami* crane will be freestanding.

Learning from the tradition of *senbazuru*

When I was at university, I tasked myself with the creation of a *senbazuru*. I was driven by completely self-serving reasons: I was in rented accommodation, and my blinds were in serious need of replacement or repair, but as it was not the most pressing priority for my landlord, after a few months I took matters into my own hands. I created my own solution to the problem in the form of a makeshift blind made out of *origami senbazuru*.

Through the process, I learned a few things.

The first was *patience* – the constant repetition of the same precise movements, over and over again, can be extremely wearing. That's not to say I didn't find it valuable – I was often able to get others involved (although their enthusiasm wore thin after a while); and it became second nature to me – something I did to clear my head at the end of a long day.

The second was the ability to *take stock and re-evaluate my goals*. I had set the task ahead of me and mapped out a timeline, but as I took part in the process, I began to realise that it wasn't quite right for my situation. In this case, the bedroom window of my little student flat was far too small to house a thousand paper cranes, so for that year I had around 250 cranes adorning it. But it was only when I had embarked on the process that I was able to see that for myself. There is a Japanese proverb that goes, 'Giving birth to a baby is easier than worrying about it'; we are often held back by the fear of doing something, but once we take action, we find that it wasn't worth the worry, the fear or the pain at all.

The third was the importance of *devotion*. The creation of *senbazuru* requires dedication on the part of its creator, whether it is helping to create good fortune for others, or for themselves. It's an investment of time and energy – but through the process, you are able to make something truly powerful and impactful, a physical expression of the respect and admiration you have for yourself and others.

How does the art of *origami* relate to compassion – to *omoiyari*? To me, whenever I see a collection of a thousand paper cranes, particularly at sporting events or weddings, the phrase 'It takes a village' springs to mind. These paper crafts are so much more than the sum of their parts – they are a physical representation of hope, happiness and goodwill. They make me think of how many people have rallied to support a person, a couple or a team – and how they are connected. Every single one of those paper cranes has been created with good intent, seeing a community come together in support.

09

OMAKASE

お任せ

To Entrust

THE ART OF LIFE LIES IN A CONSTANT READJUSTMENT TO OUR SURROUNDINGS.

Kakuzo Okakura, *The Book of Tea.*

Literally translated as 'I'll leave it up to you', an *omakase* meal is entirely chef's choice, meaning that the patrons will wholly entrust the chef to take them on a culinary journey.

Ordering *omakase* is like ordering *table d'hôte*, or the opposite of *à la carte*. For many, the concept might not appeal at all – especially those who are fussy about their food. *Omakase* probably isn't for the faint-hearted and it requires a bit of an open mind, and a spirit of adventure. Some dishes perhaps won't be quite to your taste, but that's the beauty of the experience – trying new things. In my opinion, it is something that everyone should try at least once in their lifetime. My favourite dishes at an *omakase* are always the ones that take me by surprise, or that I wouldn't have necessarily ordered myself.

An *omakase* dining experience is less like a meal, and more like a work of art. The chef will prepare their tools and use them to tell a story. You might go back to the same restaurant, with the same chef, on another day of the week and enjoy a completely different menu altogether. A talented chef will also adapt the dishes based on their perception of the guests, taking a holistic approach, too.

I recently accompanied someone on their first *omakase*. It was at a very intimate restaurant, with only seven seats at the counter, and we were entirely in the hands of the *sushi* chef for three hours. The experience was incredibly moving, and reminded me of how much joy I get from watching someone work in this way – creating and crafting a narrative throughout, bringing it to life through carefully honed techniques, and adapting the menus and timings according to the ingredients and seasons.

The word '*omakase*' comes from the verb *makaseru*, to entrust. Placing your trust in a stranger is a big ask – but when it pays off, it is truly magical.

EAT WELL, LIVE WELL.

Japanese proverb

Kaiseki 会席料理

If *omakase* is about entrusting the chef, who may adapt the menu based on each specific guest as they see fit, then a *kaiseki* meal is a demonstration of the chef's vision, distilled into a series of courses.

A traditional multi-course meal, a *kaiseki* is the Japanese equivalent of haute cuisine – a sequence of stunningly and painstakingly arranged courses. *Kaiseki* meals are served individually to each diner, on a tray, and follow a certain format, patterns and principles; they are also heavily influenced by seasonality, as well as regional differences in cuisine. When you see a *kaiseki* menu at a restaurant, you can usually expect a highly curated culinary experience. *Kaiseki* translates to something served 'banquet-style' and has been influenced by the types of meals served historically to the nobility.

However, *kaiseki* can also refer to a meal served to the guests at a tea ceremony – in speech and in writing, these are referred to as *cha-kaiseki*.

Kaiseki menus are the chef's interpretation of a specific moment in time, but also reflect the ingredients they are able to source, and a creative demonstration of their talents. *Kaiseki* meals usually follow a set format, as outlined below – while they wouldn't necessarily include all these courses, this is the kind of structure that you might encounter.

The Kaiseki Menu

Sakizuke – similar to a French amuse bouche, this is usually small and delicate and sets the tone for the meal; it is no more than one or two bites

Shokuzen-shu – an alcoholic beverage served with the *sakizuke*, usually either *sake* or *umeshu* (plum wine)

Suimono – a clear, light soup served in a lacquered bowl; the soup serves to cleanse the palate

Hassun – a dish that is an expression of the season, usually one type of *sashimi* (raw fish) dish with several seasonal side dishes

Mukōzuke – a sashimi selection

Yakimono – grilled dishes, often fish, but can also include seafood or meat

Takiawase – a vegetable course, often accompanied by tofu, meat or fish

Futamono – a dish served 'with a lid' or in a lidded bowl – usually a soup of some kind

Nimono – food that has been lightly simmered

Mushimono – a steamed dish, usually something like a *chawan-mushi* (a steamed savoury custard made with dashi broth)

Su-zakana – a vinegar-based, acidic dish to cleanse the palate between courses

Shiizakana – a hearty dish of some kind, like a hot pot

Gohan – a rice-based dish of some description

Mizumono – a dessert, usually fruit, traditional confectionery, ice cream or cake

Kaiseki principles

Ingredients and the method of preparation for a *kaiseki* meal will change depending on the chef and season. However, in general the meals follow a few set principles that define an authentic *kaiseki* experience. These include:

— Plating

The presentation of *kaiseki* dishes is very important. Dishes are served in a way that complements the food itself, so the type of ceramics, plates and bowls that you use are significant. The little details count. For example, you might use lacquered boxes or plates adorned with *sakura* blossom in the spring, or bowls and plates that evoke a sense of the ocean, depending on the setting. This is where *omoiyari* comes in – the chef won't just be thinking about the taste and texture of the food, but the presentation, the weight of a particular bowl in your hand – your entire experience.

— No repetition

This applies to the cooking techniques, ingredients and presentation. For example, you wouldn't have a fried-fish dish as well as a fried-vegetable course within the same meal; each cooking method – whether steaming, poaching or serving raw – will be employed by the chef only once per meal.

— No substitutions

A lot of heart and soul go into the preparation of the meal; there's probably no swapping out of dishes.

The Language of Food

There are a few specific terms you'll hear when you sit down for a meal in Japan and which you'll only encounter around food:

— **Meshiagare** – you might hear this phrase when someone is serving you food – the closest translation would be something like 'eat up', but it also invites the diner to get excited about the food in front of them. It might be the Japanese version of bon appetit. *Meshiagare!*

— **Oishii** – something delicious is *oishii*. If you want to tell someone how tasty you think a dish is, then *oishii* is the way to go.

— **Itadakimasu** – when you sit down to a Japanese meal, you might hear people around you say '*itadakimasu*' before they start. It's a polite way of acknowledging the effort that went into preparing the food; by saying '*itadakimasu*', you are indicating that you humbly receive the food in front of you.

— **Goshisousama deshita** – the literal translation of this is 'it was a feast'. You say this after you've finished eating, as a way of paying respect to the meal you've just devoured.

Okonomiyaki お好み焼き

If *omakase* is chef's choice, then the antonym is *okonomi* – you get to choose what to order. The culinary embodiment of *okonomi* is a savoury Japanese pancake. Some people refer to it as 'Japanese pizza', and it's called *okonomiyaki* (meaning 'cooked as you like') because you can pretty much put whatever you want into the batter. It was a staple of mine during university, and it's great for using up leftovers.

The base remains consistent, but it's the things you can add before you fry it that give it that little personalised twist. It's great if you are cooking for different dietary requirements, which is why it was such a good dish to make at university. You can live with a vegetarian, a pescatarian and a carnivore and pretty much all eat the same meal with slight tweaks and variations. I like a bit of surf-'n'-turf, so my personal preference is bacon (or pancetta) with some prawns, scallops or mussels in my batter.

If you can, try to get your hands on some *okonomiyaki* sauce – it makes all the difference. You can usually find this in an Asian supermarket, but if you don't live near one, you can try the cheat version instead, mixing equal parts ketchup, Worcestershire sauce and soy sauce with just a little bit of honey to reduce acidity.

Okonomiyaki

As a rule of thumb, it's one tablespoon of flour to every egg in the batter. The sesame oil and soy sauce aren't strictly necessary, but they do give the dish a bit more depth of flavour.

For the pancakes
4 eggs
1 teaspoon soy sauce
1 teaspoon sesame oil
4 tablespoons plain flour
pinch of salt and pepper
2 spring onions
300g cabbage
oil (vegetable or sunflower)

Sauces and toppings
Okonomiyaki sauce (or the cheat version, see p.197)
mayonnaise
aonori (seaweed)
beni shoga (pickled ginger)
katsuobushi (dried *bonito* flakes)

To make the pancakes, whisk the 'wet' items – the eggs, soy sauce, sesame oil, along with the flour and pinch of salt until the batter is smooth.

Slice the spring onions and cut the cabbage into thin strips, almost like ribbons, then add to the batter. This is the base you will be working off – think of it as a canvas. Next, you can customise it a little, adding any fillings or extras you want (or keep it plain). These

fillings go into the batter, before you fry it up as pancakes – a bit like adding chocolate chips to a traditional American-style pancake batter; you're just adding, say, seafood into your cabbage-filled pancake base instead.

Once you've put your spin on it, heat a little oil in a frying pan. I like to make one massive pancake, the kind that fills the pan; others like to make smaller ones. Either way, pour the desired amount of batter into the frying pan and wait for it to bubble on top.

Next, flip it over and fry, so that both sides are golden brown.

Transfer to a plate covered with kitchen paper, to get rid of the excess oil.

To serve, pour on a little of the *okonomiyaki* sauce, along with some mayonnaise drizzled on top as well. I also like sprinkling *aonori* (dried green seaweed), some *beni shoga* (pickled ginger) and *katsuobushi* (dried *bonito* flakes) on top, for an added kick.

Okonomiyaki fillings

- Seafood (shrimp, calamari, scallops, mussels, octopus, fishcakes)
- *Shiso* leaves
- Rice cakes
- Kimchi
- Bean sprouts
- Sweet potato
- Cheese
- Pork belly or bacon
- Anything you like; get creative – my mum puts avocado in hers

Drink Up!

As with food and dining, in Japan there are several rules and specific rituals around where and how to drink. Drinks are always decanted, and you never pour your own (or allow your companions to pour theirs) – as a gesture of hospitality, your friends pour your drink and you reciprocate. For the first round, it's polite for everyone to drink the same thing – and when raising glasses, the glass of the most senior person (whether in age or rank) should be the highest.

The Lingo

If you're planning a night out on the town, it might be useful to have these phrases up your sleeve:

— **Nomikai** – a drinking party
— **Izakaya** – the Japanese equivalent of a tapas bar; an informal bar that serves small appetisers and food
— **Kanpai** – meaning 'dry cup', *kanpai* is the Japanese equivalent of cheers! *Salud! Prost! Santé! Skål!*
— **Otsumami** – a little snack you might have along with a glass of *sake*

The word '*sake*' in Japanese refers to alcohol; what most people consider to be sake is actually *nihonshu*, a Japanese alcohol made from rice. In addition to *nihonshu*, beer is extremely popular, as well as *happoshu*, a malt-flavoured beverage. *Chu-hai* are alcopops made from *shochu*, a barley spirit. *Umeshu* is a Japanese plum wine – my grandmother makes her own in the summer months. Japanese whiskeys are also among some of the best in the world; I have a very nice bottle of Yamazaki waiting to be opened on a special occasion.

Every culture has its own set of culinary traditions. Nothing brings us together quite like a meal – and whether it's popping the kettle on for a friend after a long shift at work, or labouring over a homemade sourdough loaf, it's a simple way of showing the ones you love that you care.

Yet it's not just about what you prepare for others, but being mindful about what and how you consume, too. The approach one would take when having an *omakase* or a *kaiseki* meal, brings this dynamic to the fore – you are being performed to, in a sense. You are putting your trust in another person to make the decisions for you. They might push your boundaries. It might be unpleasant. But it also might surprise and delight you – it's a bit of a gamble. The undeniable fact is that the chef will have approached their craft with care, thought and *omoiyari*. While it might be a highly curated experience, in reality it's not so different from a parent who might prepare a meal for their child, or a group of university housemates trying to cobble together a meal based on what's currently on offer. It requires you to be imaginative, flexible, and sometimes creative.

Showing appreciation for food and, in particular, the journey it took to get to you, is something that could benefit all of us. Where did the ingredients come from? What skills were necessary to turn them into the meal in front of you? What inspired the chef? These are some questions that we can all ask ourselves. And even if it's a meal thrown together in a rush, we must remember to take the time to appreciate and savour each moment, keep an open mind and be creative, making more conscious and informed choices.

At its core, *omakase* is about harnessing the power of food and drink to build trust – in ourselves, and in each other.

SAKE REVEALS THE TRUE HEART.

Japanese proverb

CONCLUSION

A JOURNEY OF A THOUSAND MILES BEGINS WITH A SINGLE STEP.

Japanese proverb

Conclusion: What Can *Omoiyari* Bring Us?

I'm often guilty of this myself – but people are quick to anger. A familiar situation for many of us might be getting stuck behind a group of tourists as we're rushing to an appointment or being impatient as we wait for our morning latte. It's easy to become irritated, or to be curt, or to try to find another way to forge ahead.

Patience is like any other habit – it has to be practised. Many spiritual leaders spend their entire lives devoted to this; it is very much a process, part of a wider journey. *Jiji*, my grandfather, spent years tending to that small orange tree I mentioned earlier, in his garden in Kamakura. Every weekend, he would care for it, and although it would flower beautifully, it never bore fruit while he was alive. The fact that he never got to see it flourish was a small tragedy, but the tree was, in fact, a selfless gift, made all the more poignant when, after he passed, we finally got to enjoy the fruits of his labour, as well as being able to feel his presence even when he wasn't there.

Seven years after he passed away, my grandmother Motoko finally decided to sell their big house. It felt incredibly empty for her to be there alone, and it was quite remote; she now divides her time between Tokyo and an apartment in Kamakura in the old town. In many ways, that house in Kamakura was my childhood home. As I moved around every few years, it was a constant in my life, and it felt like I was beginning to grieve all over again.

My grandmother also felt the same loss, but we were both incredibly happy when a particular couple came to see the property – Japanese grandparents, with their two half-British granddaughters. For me, this was the perfect end to the story, and really evoked a sense of *mono no aware* – the transience of what makes a home and the nature of loss – but also a feeling of happiness for the new beginnings for the house we all loved so much. There were others interested in the property, but in the end, it was about honouring the past, while forging a new future. The decision was ultimately made with *omoiyari* – a feeling of respect and a desire for another family, just like ours, to love and cherish that home as much as we had.

We can all benefit from *omoiyari*, not only in the present, but future generations as well. How can we be more considerate? What kind of place are we leaving behind for those who come after us? Rather than personal profit, it is crucial, in the spirit of *omoiyari*, that we make choices and decisions with people and the planet in mind.

So how can we do this? Through the smallest actions. If you see a group of tourists, point them in the right direction, or tell them about a local place that they might have missed. Offer to carry someone's suitcase up a flight of stairs on the underground. Buy that coffee for the person behind you in line at a shop. Clean up after yourself, even if your football team has had a historic win, and all you want to do is celebrate and go a bit wild. It doesn't have to be a grand gesture – just a small promise to be the most compassionate version of yourself that you can be.

A SHORT TEMPER LEADS TO A LOSS OF SPIRIT.

Japanese proverb

About the Author

Erin Niimi Longhurst is a half-Japanese, half-British writer and the author of *Japonisme: Ikigai, forest bathing, wabi-sabi and more*. She is a director at a digital agency, working with purpose-led organisations to help them tell stories more effectively online. She has a degree in Social Anthropology from the University of Manchester, and currently splits her time between London and New York.

Glossary

Amime (網目) A stitch design used in *sashiko*-style stitching, which evokes the image of fishing nets; usually created with white thread

Aonori (青海苔) Green seaweed, often used as a topping in cooking, most commonly on *okonomiyaki* pancakes

Arigata-meiwaku (ありがためいわく) A Japanese portmanteau to describe something that someone does for you which, while filled with good intentions and coming from a good place, potentially overcomplicates things

Baba (ばあば) A Japanese nickname for grandmother, similar to 'Nana' in English

Beni shoga (紅生姜) A red pickled ginger, often used as a topping

Bon Odori (盆踊り) A traditional summer dance to welcome the spirits of the dead during the Bon Festival

Boro (ぼろ) A style of clothing made with patchwork, often dyed with indigo; deriving from the word '*boro-boro*', *boro* clothing would be passed down through generations

Boro-boro (ぼろぼろ) Something that is tattered, or in need of repair, such as a torn shirt or something scruffy

Bushido (武士道) The way of the warrior, a *samurai* code of honour

Chado (茶道) Japanese tea ceremony, also referred to sometimes as *sado*

Chitose ame (千歳飴) 'Thousand-year candy' – a treat given to children during their *Shichi-Go-San* celebration, symbolising a healthy life and longevity

Chugi (忠義) Loyalty, a virtue of the *Bushido* code

Engawa (縁側) An extension to one side of a Japanese-style house – a wooden strip of flooring, usually facing a yard or garden; an *engawa* serves as a passageway and sitting space, similar to a veranda

Engi naoshi（演技直し）
Changing one's luck through positive incantations, or 'omen fixing'; similar to the concept of manifesting

Fugen jikkō (不言実行) – A Japanese idiom, which translates to 'actions over words'.

Furikake (振り掛け) Japanese seasoning, frequently served with rice, vegetables or fish; it is often made with seaweed and *bonito* flakes

Furoshiki (風呂敷) A type of Japanese wrapping cloth, traditionally used to transport clothes, gifts or other goods

Futamono (蓋物) A dish served 'with a lid', or in a lidded bowl (usually a soup of some kind) – it's a course in *kaiseki*-style food

Genki (元気) Lively, cheerful, in good spirits; a good energy

Gi (義) Justice, a virtue of the *Bushido* code

Gohan (御飯) A rice-based course

Goshisousama deshita (ご馳走さまでした) The literal translation of this is: 'It was a feast'; you would say this after finishing eating, as a way of paying respect to the meal you've just devoured

Hana wa sakuragi, hito wa bushi (花は桜木人は武士) 'Among flowers, the cherry blossom; among men, the warrior' – a Japanese proverb meaning that as cherry blossoms are considered foremost among flowers, the *samurai* are considered foremost among people

Hanami (花見) Enjoying the transient beauty of flowers during cherry-blossom season

Hara hachi bu (腹八分目) A phrase that means to eat until you are 80 per cent full; a Japanese approach to consuming food in moderation

Harae (祓) The term for ritual purification or cleansing in the Shinto tradition

Hassun (八寸) A course in *kaiseki* cooking – an expression of the season; usually one type of *sashimi* (raw fish) dish with several seasonal side dishes

215

Ha-to (ハート) The shape of a love heart

Hibakusha (被爆者) A word for someone affected by the atomic bombing of Hiroshima and Nagasaki

Hoikuen (保育園) A Japanese nursery school

Ichariba chode (いちゃりばちょーでー) An Okinawan saying, meaning, 'Though we meet but once, even by chance, we are friends for life'

Ichi-go ichi-e (一期一会) 'One time, one meeting'; about treasuring every moment, as it cannot be repeated ever again

Ichinichiippo (一日一歩) A Japanese proverb meaning, 'One day, one step' – taking things slowly, over a long period of time

Ikebana (生け花) The Japanese art of flower arranging

Ikigai (生き甲斐) Your life's purpose

Imikotoba (忌み言葉) Taboo words

Itadakimasu (いただきます) A polite way to acknowledge, at the start of a meal, the effort that went into preparing it; by saying

'*itadakimasu*', you are saying that you humbly receive the food in front of you

Itaidoshin (異体同心) A Japanese proverb, meaning, 'Different body, same mind'

Izakaya (居酒屋) The Japanese equivalent of a tapas bar – an informal bar that serves small appetisers and food

Jaku (寂) Tranquillity, a key tenet of Japanese tea ceremony

Jiji (じいじ) A Japanese nickname for grandfather

Jin (仁) Compassion, a virtue of the *Bushido* code

Jisei (自制) Character and self-control – a virtue of the *Bushido* code

Kachou fuugetsu (花鳥風月) The characters for this are flower, bird, wind, moon – 花鳥風月 – but the meaning behind this sentiment is around experiencing the beauty of nature, and learning about yourself in the process

Kaiseki (会席) The Japanese equivalent of what the French might call haute cuisine – a sequence of stunningly and painstakingly arranged courses

Kaizen (改善) Meaning 'good change', this is a concept where small, incremental changes take place, leading to continuous improvement in systems and processes

Kanpai *(乾杯)* Meaning 'dry cup', *kanpai*, is the Japanese equivalent of cheers! Salud! Prost! Santé! Skål! If you hear it, be sure to drink up

Katsuobushi (鰹節) Dried and fermented skipjack tuna flakes, used to flavour *dashi* (Japanese stock) and in *furikake* (rice seasoning)

Kawaakari (川明かり) The reflection of light on a river in darkness

Kei (敬) Respect – a key tenet of Japanese tea ceremony

Keigo (敬語) Respectful, honorific language, often used in a business context

Keiro no hi (敬老の日) Respect for the Aged Day

Kimono (きもの/着物) A traditional Japanese garment or clothing; an example of *wafuku*

Kintsugi (金継ぎ) The art of mending broken ceramic with golden lacquer, often seen in tea ceremony; the repaired object is considered to be more beautiful and interesting as a result of its flaws

Kirei (綺麗) The word can be used interchangeably to mean 'clean' as well as 'beautiful'

Kirigami *(切り紙)* A type of *origami* that *does* require cutting with scissors, but typically not the use of glue, to create the final structure

Kokoro (心) The heart and the mind; there is no mind/body/spirit division – in *kokoro*, the heart and the mind are linked

Kokoroire *(心入れ)* Doing something wholeheartedly, with absolute devotion – usually the state of mind people try to achieve when performing tea ceremony

Kotatsu (炬燵) A type of low table covered with a *futon*; also *the* cosiest place in the world during the winter months

Kotodama (言霊) The spiritual power of words

Kusudama (薬玉) A type of modular *origami*, created by combining several individual pieces (usually flowers) to form a spherical shape

Makaseru (任せる) To entrust or put your faith in someone else to do something for you

Makoto (誠) Honesty, a virtue of the *Bushido* code

Meiyo (名誉) Honour, a virtue of the *Bushido* code

Meshiagare *(召し上がれ)* You might hear this phrase when someone is serving you food – it's the Japanese version of bon appetit and the closest translation might be something like 'eat up'; but it also invites the diner to get excited about the food in front of them

Mizumono (水物) A dessert, usually fruit, traditional confectionery, ice cream or cake

Mono no aware (物の哀れ*)* The bittersweet nature of being, an acute awareness of transience, a melancholic look at mortality – a feeling of poignant appreciation and self-awareness

Mottainai (勿体無い) A sense of regret over waste, or for things not meeting their full potential

Mukōzuke (向付) A *sashimi* selection

Mushimono (蒸物) A steamed dish, usually something like a *chawan-mushi* (a steamed savoury custard made with *dashi* broth)

Natsukashii (なつかしい) A feeling of nostalgia

Nimono (煮物) Food that has been lightly simmered

Nomikai *(飲み会)* A drinking party

Nori (海苔) Japanese seaweed, used in cooking; also the name of the author's beloved cat

Nuigurumi byouin (ぬいぐるみ病院) A hospital for stuffed toys

Obi (帯，おび) A sash or belt, worn with a traditional Japanese *kimono*

Obon (お盆) A Buddhist summer festival to honour the spirits of one's ancestors

Ochugen (お中元) Usually given between 1 and 15 July, this is

a mid-year present for people you might be indebted to (say, relatives, your doctor or physician, teachers, clients or your employers)

Oishii (美味しい) Something delicious is *oishii*

Okara (雪花菜) The soybean by-product of tofu or soy milk, used in Japanese cooking

Okonomi (お好み) The opposite of *omakase*-style dining – you get to choose what you order

Okonomiyaki (お好み焼き) A savoury Japanese pancake, made with cabbage as a base ingredient

Omakase (お任せ) 'I'll leave it up to you' – a style of ordering at a restaurant, whereby the customer will entrust the chef to put together a meal, usually seasonal

Omiyage (お土産) A gift or souvenir that you give to friends, colleagues and family when you've come back from a trip

Omoi (思い) The way people think, or their feelings, emotions, sentiments or desire

Omoi (重い) Heavy, or weighted

Omoide (思い出) Means, loosely, 'thoughts that have left'; memories or recollections

Omoiyari (思いやり) Anticipating the needs of others in an altruistic way; the art of selfless compassion – doing things for the enjoyment and comfort of others without the expectation of anything in return

Omotenashi (おもてなし) The art of selfless hospitality

Onkochishin (温故知新) Retaining the past to understand the future

Origami (折り紙) The Japanese art of paper folding

Orizuru (折鶴) Folded paper crane

Oseibo (お歳暮) The gift you might give to those you are indebted to at the end of the year, usually from early to mid-December

Osouji (大掃除) A ritual deep clean of your home, usually done at year's end, so you are all ready for the New Year

Otsumami *(おつまみ)* A little snack you might have along with a glass of *sake*

Rei (礼) Respect – a virtue of the

Bushido code

Reiwa (令和) Interpreted to mean 'beautiful harmony', this is the Imperial period that began on 1 May 2019, with the ascension of Emperor Naruhito to the Chrysanthemum throne; the previous reign, the Heisei era, ended with the abdication of Emperor Akihito on 30 April 2019

Sake kasu (酒粕) By-product of *sake* production, used to marinate fish or season vegetables

Sakiori (裂織) A type of woven fabric, made from scraps or residual materials held together using yarn

Sakizuke (先付) A little bite, similar to a French amuse bouche and usually served with an alcoholic beverage of some kind

Samurai (侍) 'One who serves' – men of noble birth who were Japanese warriors

Sashiko (刺し子) A type of decorative stitching, used to reinforce materials that have been impacted by wear and tear; *sashiko* sewing techniques are often geometric in style,

making repairs aesthetically pleasing through the use of 'little stitches' (the translation of the term)

Sei (清) Purity, a key tenet of Japanese tea ceremony

Seijin no hi – Coming of Age Day (成人の日) The day when young people mature into adulthood, and celebrate with a ceremony at an official building; there is also an after-party

Seijin shiki (成年礼) Coming-of-age ceremony, which takes place at an official building of some kind, followed by a temple visit

Seikestu (清潔) Standardising, adding structure

Seiri (整理) Sorting and organising

Seiso (清掃) Shining, polishing, cleaning

Seiton (整頓) Setting in order

Seiza (正座 or 正坐) Literally 'proper sitting', this is the Japanese term for the standard formal traditional way of sitting in Japan

Senbazuru (千羽鶴) A thousand paper *origami* cranes

Sento (銭湯) Communal bathhouses

Shichi-Go-San (七五三) A traditional rite of passage for children aged seven, five and three

Shiizakana (強肴) A hearty course in *kaiseki* cooking – something like a hot-pot course

Shinrin-yoku (森林浴) Forest bathing – the practice of immersing yourself in nature

Shinto (神道) A Japanese indigenous religion dating from the early eighth century, incorporating the worship of ancestors, spirits and a belief in sacred power (*kami*) in both animate and inanimate things

Shinzou (心臓) The Japanese word for heart – when referring to the organ

Shitsuke (躾) Self-discipline

Shokuzen-shu (食前酒) An alcoholic beverage served with the *sakizuke*, usually either *sake* or *umeshu*

Suimono (吸物) A clear, light soup served in a lacquered bowl

Susu-harai (煤払い) Ritual cleaning ceremony

Sumimasen (すみません) The most useful word in the Japanese language; depending on context, it can mean 'excuse me', 'thank you' or 'I'm sorry'

Su-zakana (酢肴) A vinegar-based, acidic palate cleanser between courses

Takiawase (煮合) A vegetable course, often accompanied by tofu, meat or fish

Tanki wa sonki (短気は損気) A Japanese proverb, meaning a short temper leads to a loss of spirit, or comes at a detriment

Tatami (畳) Woven straw flooring

Tate-waku (竪沸く) A stitch design used in *sashiko*, evoking an image of rising steam; usually woven with white thread

Teinei (丁寧) Approaching something with polite conscientiousness

Temizuya (手水舎) Shinto water ablution pavilion for a ceremonial purification rite known as *temizu*

Tenugui (手拭い) A thin cotton hand towel, often given as a gift

Tokonoma (床の間) A recess or

alcove in a Japanese house, typically a few inches above floor level, used for displaying flowers, pictures and ornaments

Toro nagashi (灯籠流し) Paper lanterns are floated across a river, usually to close the *Bon* festival; the significance behind this is to guide the souls of the departed back to the spirit world

Toshigami (年神) The deity or spirits of the coming year; people might perform *osouji* in their homes to welcome *toshigami* into the home and bring good luck for the New Year

Tsundoku (積ん読) Books you purchase but that end up unread, just taking up space in your home (hopefully not this one)

Tsuru (鶴) Japanese crane

Tsurukame (鶴亀) Crane and tortoise – a positive incantation to ward off bad luck

Wa (和) Harmony and cohesion

Wabi-sabi (侘寂) A Japanese aesthetic and worldview that promotes the acceptance of transience, impermanence and

imperfection

Wafu (和風) Japanese style

Wafuku (和服) Japanese-style clothing, like *kimonos*

Washi (和紙) Japanese paper

Washitsu (和室) A Japanese-style room

Yakimono (焼物) Grilled dishes; often fish, but can also include seafood or meat

Yakiniku (焼き肉) Grilled meat

Yarai (矢来) A stitch design used in *sashiko*, evoking the image of a bamboo fence; usually sewn with white thread

Yu (勇) Courage – a virtue of the *Bushido* code

Zakka (雑貨) Miscellaneous goods; or a wider cultural aesthetic, with a focus on finding the beauty in the ordinary

Acknowledgments

Thank you to everyone who made this book possible – in particular the team at HarperCollins and my incredible family. I'd also like to thank the eggs (Carmen Barrera, Ella Paskett, Nicole Dulieu), Tom Durrands, Lea Main-Klingst, Harriet Morris, Matthew Millett, Amy, Mina, Dad, Rosie, Clement and Katie.

A special thanks to my amazing mother, Eriko; my grandmother Motoko, and my aunts, Junko and Taeko. I'd also like to acknowledge the debt of gratitude I owe to several other women in my life – my grandmother Gilly, and my aunts – Hilary, Jo and Lucy.

Thank you to those who shared their stories of *omoiyari*, or the spirit of *omotenashi* with me for this book: Emma Cooke, Fatma Arslan, Nicole Tamer, Victoria Nightingale, Thach Quach, Chris Baldwin, Lexi Quint and all the others who told their stories too – *domo arigato*.

Endnotes

1. https://web.archive.org/web/20110601034605/http://www.un.org/wcm/webdav/site/climatechange/shared/Documents/SpeechMaathai.pdf
2. https://nypost.com/2016/03/14/japanese-tour-guides-are-cleaning-the-filthy-streets-of-paris-themselves/
3. https://www.japantimes.co.jp/news/2019/04/01/national/politics-diplomacy/japan-read-ies-announce-name-new-era/#.XlMeJhP7Sv4
4. https://www.who.int/countries/jpn/en/

Picture credits

pp4-5, 16, 19, 20, 24, 25, 26, 27, 29, 32, 34-5, 36, 39, 40, 41, 42, 45, 48, 50, 54-5, 56, 59, 60, 66, 71, 74-5, 76, 83, 85, 87, 89, 91, 94-5, 101, 102, 103, 105, 109, 110, 112, 113, 114-5, 119, 120, 123, 136-7, 154-5, 159, 161, 167, 168-9, 173, 176, 179, 180, 183, 186-7, 190, 194, 199, 200, 204, 219 © Shutterstock.com; p8, 10-11, 46, 81, 92, 96, 98-9, 133, 149, 196, 208, 211 © Robert McConkey; p13, 147, 163, 188 © Ella Kiyomi Dobson; p15 Gabriel Forsberg on Unsplash; p28 Mint Images/Alamy Stock Photo; p31 David Emrich on Unsplash; p43 J Marshall-Tribaleye Images/Alamy Stock Photo; p50 Annie Spratt on Unsplash (top), Milada Vigerova on Unsplash (bottom) p53, 101 (top) Linh Le on Unsplash; p65 Minh Pham on Unsplash; p72 Chandra Oh on Unsplash; p111 Joshua Sazon on Unsplash; p116 Alex Alvarez on Unsplash; p124-125 © Daj/GettyImages; p126 Free To Use Sounds on Unsplash; p130 Meric Dagli on Unsplash; p135, 212, 213 © Erin Niimi Longhurst; p141 Hardik Pandya on Unsplash; p142 Dale Scogings on Unsplash; p144 Masaaki Komori on Unsplash; p151 Ryoji Iwata on Unsplash; p153 © Image Navi – Sozaijiten/Alamy Stock Photo; p156 Jeremy Kieran on Unsplash; p175 Hideki Nishiyama on Unsplash; p203 Tom Crew on Unsplash; p205 Nicki Eliza Schinow on Unsplash.